FOR THE HOME
FOR YOURSELF
FOR GIFTS

IDEAS GALORE!

Keep an eye out for design ideas and you'll find them all around you . . . in your house, your garden, even on objects and toys! Just to prove that sources for designs are everywhere, we've coupled each original inspiration here with its offspring.

The trim on a minipurse inspired the crocheted ruffle on our camisole.

Adapt a Simplicity embroidery transfer to make stencil flowers bloom like these.

If your child has a favorite animal friend, stitch a knitted pet pouch right onto her hooded cover-up.

Plant some greenery on an apron bib! Here, the ceramic planter design comes to life once again in cross-stitch.

Fabricate some homey feelings — appliqué your dream-house on a charming pillow.

Use native crafts to add an ethnic flavor to your fashions, like our felt vest inspired by a bold Navajo wall hanging.

DESIGN DECISIONS

A little creativity can make your sewing projects something extra-special. What do we mean by special? It can be as simple as braiding textured yarns together to create a unique closure . . . or patchworking a decorative border along a hem edge. All it takes is a little thought and some decision-making. For instance, where will you find designs? How and where will you use them? And most important—what method will you use? We've eliminated a lot of the guesswork. This chapter will answer all your questions and get you started; the rest of the book will give you the how-to's and the inspiration to whip up fabulous projects. All of the instructions are quick and easy to follow for decorating fashions, accessories or home furnishings, with shortcut methods for many traditionally time-consuming crafts. Sew Something Special . . . why not start right now!

A

B

C

WHAT DESIGN?

The first step is choosing a design. Iron-on transfers are a handy source of designs. Whether you embroider, appliqué or paint, Simplicity offers a selection of patterns with iron-on designs and instructions (A).

Don't stop with purchased transfers... create your own original design! Sources of inspiration are endless! Just look around you—you'll be amazed at what you can find in your own home. Here are just a few ideas:

The kitchen—A fancy dish towel, china patterns, utensils, a ceramic tile, even package labels can be adapted and used to decorate garments and accessories.

The toy chest—Toys and picture books are open to many whimsical interpretations. Convert animal shapes into amusing pillows, murals, appliqués or pockets for children.

Your own wardrobe—The border on your favorite scarf can become a needlework belt design. Or try a lacy embroidered handkerchief, fancy pillowcase or crocheted bag as a source of trim ideas.

Museums and department stores—A work of art or an Indian wall hanging might inspire you to try your hand at a modern adaptation.

Lettering—Nothing identifies a fashion as your own like a monogram! For clear lettering, use stencils or printed letters. Consider repeating your own monogram as a design around a needlepoint belt (B).

Printed material—Cut illustrations or photos from seed packets, cards or magazines. Trace and transfer to fabric; then use as a needlework design for a pillow (C).

Your own house—Cottage or castle, picture it in appliqué, needlepoint, machine embroidery or in collage.

Travel—Whether you go across the country or across the ocean, you're sure to encounter all sorts of inspiration for designs. Made up into clothes or home fashions, they'll be your favorite souvenirs!

Design ideas are everywhere! See the photos opposite for just a few of the design sources we found nearby. Then, you can train yourself to notice and adapt the many design ideas that are all around you.

COLOR

You'll find that a few general color rules make the work of planning your design easier. Keep them in mind when you're selecting designs, supplies and fabrics. Then take a look at the photographs throughout the book for lots of ideas to spark your imagination.

A

• When personalizing a garment, consider the color of the fabric as well as those which are complimentary to you. For example, if the garment will be made in multi-colored fabric, choose one of the dominant colors for your decoration (A). On solid fabric, use a contrasting color (or colors), such as red on white, for design impact; or use a closely related shade for a subtle effect.

• When adding a special touch to an accessory for your home, relate the colors you'll use to the color scheme in the room. In a room with several colors, choose one of the dominant colors for your project. In a room of neutrals, select a shade or tint of one of the colors—or choose a bold contrast for accent.

DESIGN PLACEMENT

Now, you've got a great design idea. Where should it go on the garment? Certain areas of a garment are more easily enhanced than others—cuffs, collars, pockets, yokes, waistlines and hemlines are naturals (A). When in doubt, use the strongest design lines as a guide and play them up. Shaped seams, an unusual neckline or closure are some of the features you may want to emphasize (B). For the most appealing results, accent only one or two main features, such as an interesting yoke and pocket flaps. In home accessories, design placement can be more dramatic, with larger areas of decoration. Hem, border or corner decoration of tablecloths, placemats and curtains is attractive and easy to do (C).

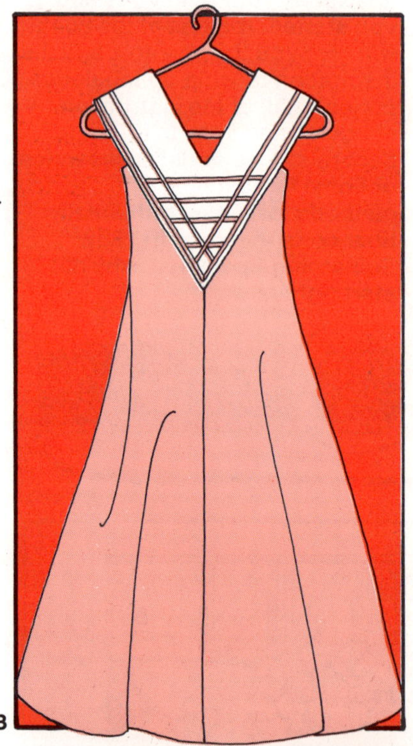

B

C

DESIGN SIZE

Having made most of the important design decisions, you must now find a suitable size for your design. If the design needs enlarging or reducing, there are several ways to do this.

D

The easiest method is to take the design to a photostat house where it can be enlarged or reduced to the desired size for a few dollars.

However, you can easily do the job yourself by using the folded paper method. Draw a square on paper around the design and fold paper horizontally and vertically to form smaller squares. Cut a second square piece of paper, the size you want the design to be, and fold into the same number of squares. Draw design onto second piece of paper, using a sharp pencil. Work square by square for accuracy (D).

DESIGN TRANSFER

To position the design, fold design paper and fabric in half lengthwise, then crosswise. Crease paper, mark fold in fabric with pins. Center creases over pin markings and tape design to fabric (E).

E

TRANSFER METHODS

The following methods are suitable for transferring designs to fabric. Consider fabric type and design choice to determine best method.

Iron-on Transfers: This is one of the

A

easiest methods for transferring embroidery designs. The Simplicity iron-on transfer patterns contain complete instructions. Follow them exactly for best results.

Test the transfer pattern for clarity of imprint. Pin or tape a scrap of your fabric, right side up, on an ironing board or tabletop protected by a bath towel. The transferred design usually will show more clearly if you place aluminum foil under fabric before pressing. Cut out a trial motif, leaving a margin. Tape, pin or baste motif, print side down, on fabric. Test iron temperature by pressing straight down on motif. Do not glide iron; hold in one place or design will smudge (A). If iron is warm enough, the print will be clear. Now test removability of the stamped motif by washing (if fabric is washable), or with a good cleaning fluid. If the design isn't clear, use a white or lead pencil to make the design lines more visible. If your test was successful, you can transfer the design to your fabric as for test motif. Some transfers can be re-used.

Transfer Pencil: Transfer pencils are sold in needlecraft and art supply stores. Trace a mirror image of the design on the back of the design paper. Then transfer design to fabric with a hot iron, following the Iron-on Transfer hints above.

Sheer Fabric Transfer: Place the fabric over the design paper and trace the design directly onto the fabric with a colored pencil.

Napped or Pile Fabric Transfer: The pile or nap on velvet, corduroy, terry cloth and other napped fabrics makes normal transfer methods unsuitable. Transfer the design to wrong side of the fabric, and then hand-baste along design lines to

B

bring them to the right side. Or, for embroidery, transfer design onto organdy and baste to napped fabric. Embroider through both layers and remove organdy by clipping and pulling threads away (B).

Tracing Designs: A transfer design printed in dark blue ink must be traced onto a dark fabric. This way a transfer design can be used more than once. Tape fabric right side up on a hard surface. Place design on fabric. Slip dressmaker's carbon paper, waxed side down, under design. Tape in place. Transfer design by going over lines with a pencil or stylus (C). Bear down hard enough so that lines transfer. Tracing is also suitable for leather, suede, vinyl, and synthetic suede or leather.

C

Multiple Transfer: To transfer the same design several times, as for patchwork or appliqué, cut a template or master pattern. Trace design onto cardboard with carbon paper and a sharp pencil, including the seam allowances for seamed patchwork or

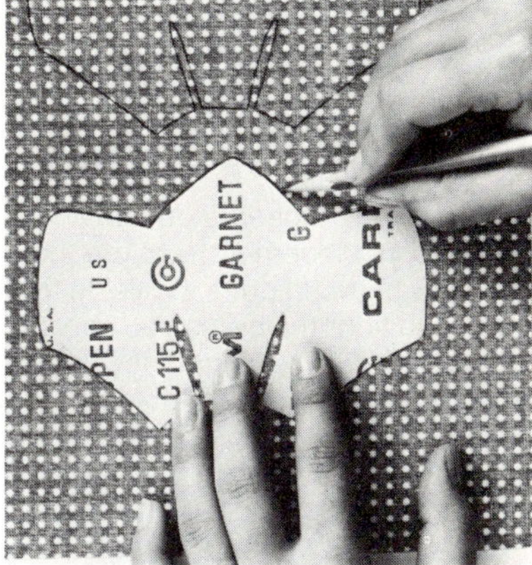

D

machine-stitched appliqués. Fused items do not need seam allowances. Cut out template with sharp scissors, mat knife or razor blade. Trace around template to transfer design to fabric (D), repeating as necessary. To keep templates from slipping, make them from sandpaper.

Canvas Transfer: For transferring a bold design onto a fine mesh canvas, use an iron-on transfer or a transfer pencil. For coarse mesh canvas, trace the design directly onto the canvas with a permanent marking pen (E). Test-mark a scrap and dampen it first to be sure the color will not bleed through when you block your work. If there are strong horizontals or verticals, be sure to place them on the straight grain of the canvas.

E

GLOSSARY OF METHODS AND MATERIALS

Once you've chosen a design and planned its placement, explore the many craft techniques available to you. Consider the crafts you can do already, or try something new! Think about those that are suitable for the project and the design. Do you like to do appliqué or quilting? Or does the design or fabric lend itself more readily to doing embroidery or needlepoint? Perhaps ribbons, beads or binding will give you the effect you're after. You might consider combining two or more decorative techniques for a real touch of genius!

While choosing a method that is pleasing to your eye, try to make it a practical choice, too. Some time-consuming techniques, such as hand embroidery, make more sense when used for accents. Others, like quilting, go quickly and can be used for an entire garment or large sections of it. Some methods work best on specific fabrics—for example, machine embroidery on opaque fabrics, tie-dyeing on sheers. If washability is a factor, this, too, should influence your selection. Rickrack, piping or machine embroidery may prove a better choice than ribbon, beads or other trims that are not easily laundered. You'll find more specific practical considerations and advice for every method in each chapter.

All other factors aside, choose the method and medium that appeals to you most, perhaps for its originality. Your craft should, after all, give you lots of pleasure!

To help you select the best method for your purposes, here's a list of craft possibilities along with simple explanations of each technique. Despite their hand-crafted look, most are accomplished with speed and ease by your sewing machine.

THE QUILT REVISITED

The centuries-old crafts of quilting, appliqué and patchwork have been updated and made simple!

Appliqué: A cut-out design of one or more fabrics sewn by hand or machine, or fused, to a background fabric. It is sometimes padded (A).

Patchwork: Pieces of fabric sewn or fused together to create a design (B). Geometric shapes such as squares, triangles and hexagons are the most common patch shapes. Random shapes combine to make crazy-quilt designs.

Quilting: Hand or machine stitching which holds two layers of fabric together with batting sandwiched in between, creating a puffy effect (A). Several stitching designs are possible— square, diamond, cartridge (B), scroll or outline quilting.

A

THOSE FABULOUS FABRICS

The marvelous fabrics available today enable you to make your garment really special without even adding any extras (A). Just learn to use fabrics imaginatively by following these suggestions.

Special Layouts: The careful placement of the pattern on your fabric in order to incorporate a distinctive fabric design into a garment or accessory. Many print fabrics, such as border, scarf, large scale or panel prints, require special layouts for the most pleasing use of the design (B). Similarly, lace borders can be placed horizontally or vertically on many garment edges to create an attractive decorative edge requiring no finishing. Special layouts can also make use of the finished hems that border sheets, towels, curtains and tablecloths.

Mixtures: An attractive combination of two or more complementary fabrics in one garment. Mixtures may be based on color, texture, design, scale or direction. When combining fabrics, be sure there is a common characteristic or unifying feature shared by the fabrics for the most appealing results. For instance, large and small checks may be combined, provided they are of the same texture or color scheme. Various colored prints may be combined if they are all of similar design or scale. When mixing fabrics, the objective is to create additional interest without sacrificing a pleasing, unified overall effect.

Leather-likes and Other Non-ravel Fabrics: Felt, blanket fabrics, melton, pseudo-suede, vinyl and leather-likes. Fabrics that do not ravel and have substantial body can be handled with simplified construction methods—the same ones used by clothing manufacturers in the interest of time and professional results on bulky fabrics. Interfacings, linings, facings, hems and traditional edge finishes are often not necessary. Without further finishing, these fabrics may be cut into self-fringe, scalloped, pinked, punched with intricate hole designs or laced together. With these versatile fabrics and updated methods, almost anything goes!

B

A

SAY IT WITH STITCHERY

Stitchery is a highly decorative medium including everything from tiny, intricate embroidery to bold, dramatic punch-needle work! Traditional stitchery demands hours of work. Now, quicker methods give the same beautiful results.

Machine Embroidery: Straight, zig-zag or other automatic decorative stitches worked by machine. Free motion embroidery is done with an embroidery hoop and without a presser foot.

Easy Hand Embroidery: Selected quick stitches sewn with six-strand embroidery floss or yarn (A). The simplicity of the stitch, its size and the thread used make these stitches a fast way to add hand embroidery to fashions. The stitches include: *Cross-Stitch,* two straight stitches crossing each other at right angles; *Blanket Stitch,* interlocking, parallel stitches; *Straight Stitch,* a simple up-and-down stitch in any length and direction; *Chain Stitch,* forming a continuous chain of loops; *Overcast Stitch,* a series of straight or slanting parallel stitches; *Running Stitch,* forming a broken line; *Stem Stitch,* the most basic outline stitch; *Lazy-Daisy Stitch,* detached loops often used for petals; *Backstitch,* another type of outline stitch; *Herringbone Stitch,* a variation of Cross-Stitch; and *Feather Stitch,* a series of open loops.

Punch-Needle Work: A quick method of inserting continuous loops of yarn into fabric with a large, needle-like tool to give a textured effect to pillows or garments (B).

Needlepoint: Embroidery done on canvas mesh with yarns or satin cord. Rug yarn on large mesh canvas in *Half Cross* or *Continental Stitch* produces *quickpoint,* less time-consuming than smaller scale needlepoint. *Bargello (Florentine Stitch)* and *Gobelin Stitch*, long stitches worked vertically over two to six meshes (C), are also faster to do.

Trapunto: Areas of decorative detail with a puffy quilted effect achieved by stuffing machine-stitched areas (D).

TERRIFIC TRIMS

Add trims to a garment or accessory for a personalized design statement! We've included only those that are easily applied by machine (E).

Appliqués: Fabric shapes applied by machine stitching or fusing. Some even iron or stick on (F).

B

C

D

E

F

Binding: Trims that conceal and decorate a raw edge in one step. Double-fold bias binding or foldover braid both have one slightly wider side for easy application (F).

Border and Top Trim: Trims with two finished edges—rickrack, ribbon, double ruffles, some laces, bands and braids (E opposite). Wide borders are usually topstitched in place along both edges. Narrow ones (middy braid or rickrack) are stitched through the center (F).

Edging: Trims with at least one decorative edge, such as fringe, piping and pre-gathered ruffles, used at any edge (neckline, collar, cuff, hem) or inserted in seams (F).

Insertion: See-through trims with two finished edges sewn onto a garment, with the fabric underneath cut away to give a transparent effect. Inserts may be placed in flat areas without darts or curved seams, such as pants legs, hems and sleeves (F).

Lacing: Strips of leather, cording, jute, shoelaces, etc. threaded through eyelets or hooks at edges or seams, or used as decorative ties or closures (F).

Trim Weaving: Ribbons or trims interwoven horizontally and vertically to create a decorative section of fabric for a garment, accessory or home furnishing item.

ADD A CRAFT

Crafts that are distant relatives of sewing are also fun ways of creating unusual accessories for your fashions and your home.

Stitch-and-Stuff: Often called soft sculpture, three-dimensional, multi-purpose items made by stitching two layers of fabric together and stuffing. Design inspiration can come from simple shapes—animals, plants, etc. Use them as pillows, wall decorations or sit-upons.

Braiding: Strands of yarn or cord intertwined in hair-braid style, used to trim edges on collars, cuffs, pillows, and for tie fastenings. Sew flat braids together to create fabric for placemats or handbags.

Crochet: Yarn or thread interlaced with a crochet hook to create dense or open lacy areas. Decoratively speaking, simple crochet lends itself beautifully to edgings, ruffles (A) and joining seams instead of stitching.

Knotting: Yarn, string, etc., tied in simple knots, sometimes combined with beads between knots. Basic knotting can produce an unusual belt or fringe for edges of a shawl or evening bag (B).

Hooking: Lengths of yarns knotted into loosely-woven fabric to produce a shag texture for wall hangings, rugs and afghans. Use hooking to accent a design area, for a shaggy look without all the work of hooking the entire item. This method uses a latch hook and precut yarn.

Knitting: Loops of yarn interlocked with a pair of knitting needles to produce a smooth or textured fabric. Paired with sewing, knitting can create surface interest, replacing fabric sections on fashions or edging home furnishing items.

Collage: A combination of several different materials—fabric, yarn, buttons, trims—cut into shapes and arranged to form a design on a backing. Materials can be stitched, glued or fused to create textural scenics or still-life designs for pictures, fashions, pillows, etc.

Button Art: Assorted sizes and shapes of buttons stitched at random or in a planned design for a unique, decorative treatment.

A

B

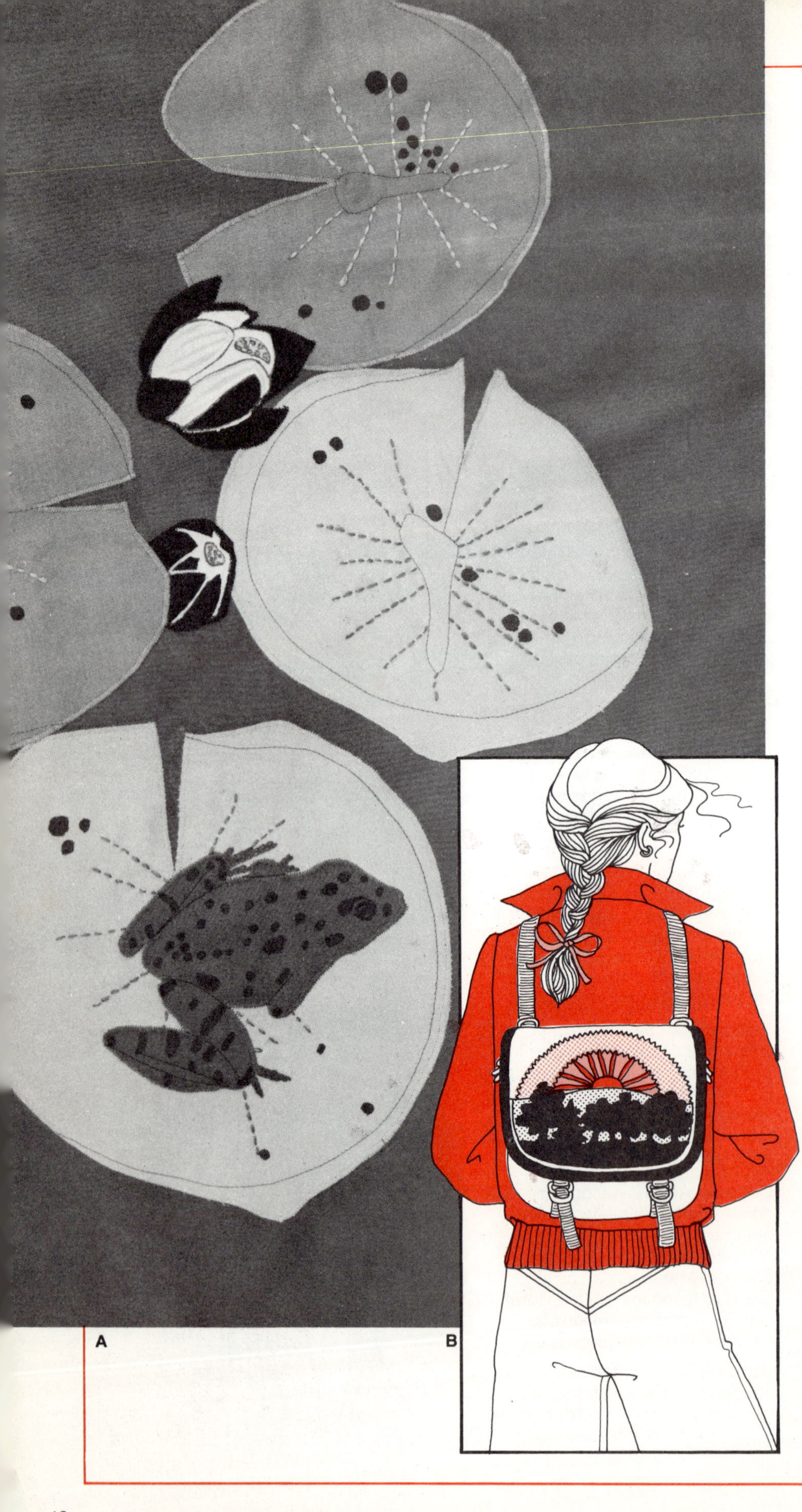

A

B

MIXED MEDIA

Sewing combines with other arts, such as painting and dyeing, to create uncommon-looking, original designs (A, B). Experiment ... try appliqué with collage, combine painting with trims, or just stencil a whole section of a garment. The principle of mixed media allows you to create endless combinations, using all sorts of design possibilities.

Painting: The application of colorfast textile paints to fabric, using felt-tip markers, tubes or jars of paint, crayons or glitter. Textile paints can create beautiful and permanent designs that are fun—and fast—to do.

Stenciling: A method of applying a design to fabric by cutting a motif out of heavy paper and painting inside the cut-out with colorfast textile paints. Designs are usually simple, repetitive shapes and may be done in one or more colors. You can make your own stencils or purchase them ready to use.

Pour-on Dyeing: A variation of tie-dyeing in which liquid dye is poured onto fabric to form stripes or chevrons. After the dyed stripes are gathered and tied off, the fabric is then dyed in the usual way. The knotted-off areas will retain the poured-on stripes while the rest of the fabric absorbs the new background color.

More Mixed Media: Once you've tried painting, stenciling and pour-on dyeing, you can go on to create your own fabulous one-of-a-kind fashions with all the techniques you can learn from this book. You'll see that trims, stitchery, patchwork, appliqué, special fabrics and crafts can all work together as mixed media for fashions, accessories and home furnishings that are really uniquely you!

TRIM

HOW-TO HAND BOOK

This book is organized to give you—and your creative instincts—maximum help. The opening chapter is full of suggestions for designs, as well as the basic know-how you'll need to get started—what methods are available, how to work with colors and fabrics, how to convert an inspiration into a design.

The next six chapters present a variety of techniques you can use to make your sewing project a truly personal expression. Each includes general directions for the techniques, with lots of clear, step-by-step diagrams and photographs. You'll also find complete instructions for making all 53 of the projects shown in the color photographs.

You'll notice that each project includes one or more ♥'s. We've added this helpful rating so you can judge the relative ease of doing each project. ♥ means quick and easy, ♥♥ means moderately fast and easy, and ♥♥♥ indicates that the project takes somewhat more time and effort. Finally, at the end of each chapter, there's a bonus page—an Idea File—of even more sew-special projects for you to make and enjoy.

THE QUILT REVISITED

CRAFT UPDATE!

Take brand-new inspiration from America's rich heritage of quilts. Patchwork, appliqué and quilting combine here to create five of the prettiest possibilities. What's more, though the ideas are traditional, the designs and methods are right now!

1 The updated quilt makes handy use of appliqué, patchwork and quilting to create this lush blend of color and design.♥♥♥

2 Plain and fancy vest is reversible. Just outline-quilt the print to create the subtle design on the solid.♥♥

3 These appliquéd overalls are a child's delight with mother duck and her colorful eggs stitched on for all the world to see!♥♥

4 Not just any hooded top, this one sports a new idea in easy appliqué. One beautiful scarf provides all the motifs you see, so decorate away!♥

5 More innovative appliqué scatters floral motifs cut from the skirt fabric along the border of this soft challis stole.♥

Instructions, pages 22-24

8065
7908
8069
8076

THE QUILT REVISITED

Appliqué or patch it, mix it or match it—then quilt the whole batch! Here are more winning ways with the elements of our modern-day quilt.

6 Traditional patchwork motifs, sewn on by machine, stand out boldly on this great cover-up apron.♥♥

7 No carpentry skills are necessary to build this pillow-house. It's all done with fabric scraps and quick-as-a-wink machine-appliqué.♥♥

8 He'll love it! All you have to do is save small scraps of wool plaids to make this handsome and unusual patchwork tie.♥

9 Western-style shirt sports patchwork on yoke and cuffs. Calico-print patches are easily fused on, then outlined with machine embroidery.♥

10 Our version of the carpetbag is done in plush textures of corduroy and downy velveteen in subtle shades. To create the patchwork we just staggered strips. Try it!♥♥

11 Our bold padded appliqué makes the basic envelope bag a special accessory.♥

How-to's pages 22-24

THE QUILT REVISITED

A quilt is a lively, warm fabric sandwich—a top, batting and backing all stitched together with a decorative design. The techniques usually associated with a quilt—patchwork and appliqué on the top and quilting through the layers—are really three distinct elements. Used alone or together, they can create beautiful clothes, home furnishings, accessories and even a quilt! Doing patchwork, appliqué and quilting by hand is the traditional method for making a quilt in leisurely fashion. But times—and life-styles—have changed. Contemporary fashions borrow inspiration from the age-old arts, but take a modern approach to methods. With the sewing machine, you gain the time and speed to make all three techniques work creatively in fashions for you and your home.

PATCHWORK

Patchwork has roots deep in history. Our great-great-grandmothers used patchwork as a way of recycling remnants of precious fabrics. Piecing together various shapes and colors, they created quilts which became prized as heirlooms and which bore such colorful names as Log Cabin, Lone Star, Drunkard's Path, Orange Peel and many others. These traditional designs have inspired our simple, modern versions which can be assembled quickly and easily, using shortcut machine stitching and fusing techniques. Patchwork is a great decorative accent on clothing—as a collar or yoke and cuffs on a shirt, for instance. And, it goes beautifully into pillows or a contemporary wall hanging.

A

B

C

DESIGNS

Sources of inspiration are endless. See Design Decisions, page 5, for ideas to help you get started. The easiest shape to work with is a square. It can be combined effectively with other squares in random multicolor prints (A) or done as a more formal alternating print-and-solid combination (B). Other good shapes are rectangles, diamonds and triangles; join these in various ways to form square or rectangular blocks (C). Graph paper and colored pencils will help you with colors and arrangements for your design. Try different shapes, colors and patterns until you come up with one that you like. The size of patch shapes or blocks should be in keeping with the detail area where they'll be used. For yokes or other small sections, 2″ (5 cm) is a good size. For large areas, 5 to 6″ (12.5 to 15 cm) blocks are more appropriate.

FABRICS

When choosing fabric, almost anything goes—cottons and cotton blends, silks and satins, velvets, stable knits, even fake (or real) furs and leathers can be used for the top or face of the patchwork or appliqué piece. Don't hesitate to mix colors, prints and textures that contrast but look right together. For additional guidance, see Color, page 6, and Fabric Mixing, page 32. Just be sure all elements—fashion fabric, batting and backing (if you're using them)—require the same care. Also, try to keep fabrics similar in weight so they will wear equally.

FIGURING YARDAGE

For a small project, you can use remnants that you have on hand. If you need to buy fabric for a large project, figure yardage this way:

1. Decide on the finished size of the project, the size of the individual shapes and the number of different fabrics you'll use. (Example: 5″ squares, six across by ten down; equal amounts of three fabrics (A).

2. Multiply the total width of all the shapes by the total length, including 1/4″ (6 mm) seam allowances if patchwork will be assembled by machine. (Example: 5½″ x 6 = 33″ total width; 5½″ x 10 = 55″ total length. 33″ x 55″ = 1815 square inches total patchwork area.)

3. Divide the total area by the number of different fabrics. (Example: 1815 ÷ 3 = 605 square inches of each fabric.)

4. To convert to yards, divide by the width of the fabric. (Example: 45″ wide. 605 ÷ 45 = 13.4″ of 45″ fabric, or about 3/8 yard (.35 m).

CUTTING

Once you've decided on your design, make a template (cutting pattern) for each patch shape, adding 1/4″ (6 mm) seam allowances all around for machine assembly. Use the templates to transfer the patch shapes to your fabric as directed on page 7. Cut out the shapes on the *traced* line. If you have a lot of patches, you can save time by cutting up to four layers of fabric at a time. Just trace the shape onto the top layer and pin through all layers to hold them as you cut.

ASSEMBLING

After cutting, assemble pieces by machine or by fusing. Fusing is easiest with irregularly shaped patches.

Seaming: Join shapes to form blocks, such as two triangles for a square block (B, C). Next, sew the blocks together, forming strips (D), and finally, join the strips. If you are assembling blocks with several pieces, begin at the center of the block and work out (E, F). Sew blocks into strips, then join the strips.

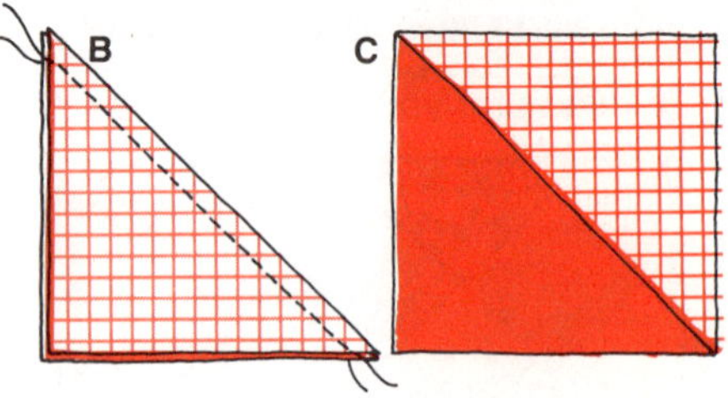

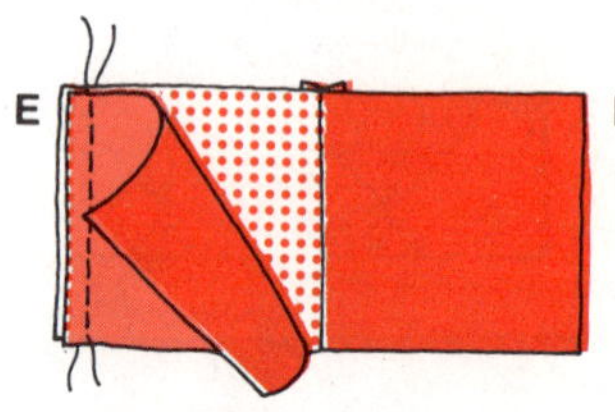

Shortcut Seaming: For squares and rectangles, use this method: First mark horizontal strips with 1/4″ (6 mm) seam allowances on the fabrics you plan to use; then, cut and seam them (G). Press seams open, then mark off vertical strips (H). To create patchwork, stagger strips, stitch seams and press open (I).

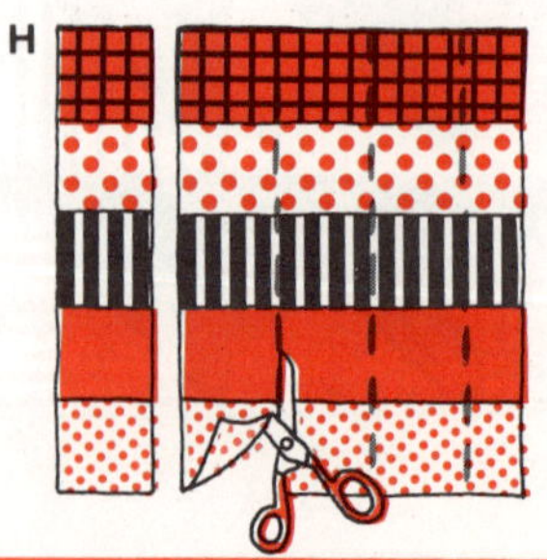

A

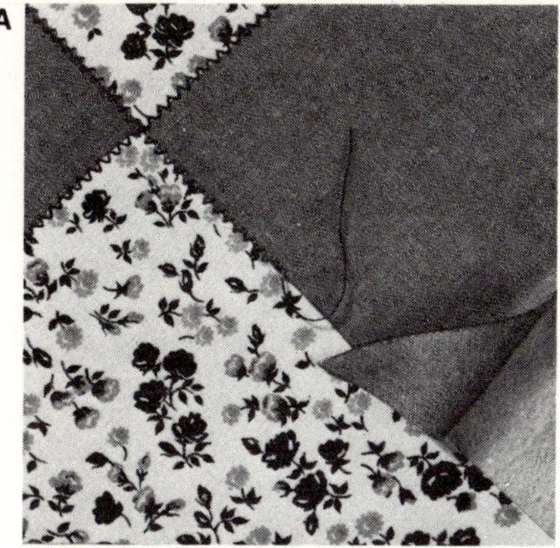

Super-Quick Patchwork: On areas like yokes, collars, and placemats, the fusing method works well and acts as an interfacing. Cut fabric shapes without seam allowances, cutting fusible web the same size and shape. Then, following manufacturer's instructions, fuse pieces to a lightweight background fabric (A), which can be part of the design, too; let it peek through here and there (B). Then satin-stitch (close zigzag) over the edges to keep them from raveling (B).

B

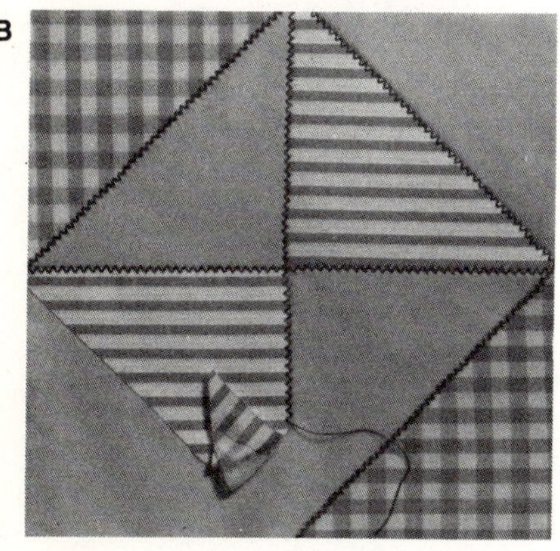

Crazy-quilt Patchwork: This variation of traditional patchwork uses irregular-shaped pieces put together at random. Our ancestors would join bits of silk, satin and velvet and then embroider over the seams with feather stitching or other fancy hand stitches. The resulting quilt would be quite handsome and elegant.

To assemble your own crazy-quilt patchwork, cut a piece of lightweight backing fabric the desired size of the finished patchwork, plus 5/8″ (1.5 cm) on all edges. Now cut patches of various fabrics and arrange them on

C

the backing. Patches may be geometric or irregular in shape, with straight or curved edges. Overlap the patches to create a variety of shapes, leaving some of the background fabric showing, if you like. Pin all patches in place, then machine-baste or fuse to the backing. Secure the patches with satin-stitching (close zigzag) or decorative stitching over all raw edges (C).

Crazy-quilt patchwork may also be done in blocks. Just cut the required number of blocks of backing fabric, adding 1/4″ (6 mm) seam allowances all around, and attach patches to each block as described above. The blocks may be identical or varied. Assemble the blocks just as you would for regular patchwork.

SEWING AND FINISHING

Now that you've finished creating your patchwork fabric, you can use it to make garments or home furnishings—pillows, wall hangings, tablecloths, quilts. To keep seams of patchwork from coming apart, staystitch 1/2″ (1.3 cm) from the outer edges or cut a lightweight backing and staystitch the patchwork to it. For garments, lay out pattern pieces on the straight grain of the patchwork according to your plan (D), pin and cut out; then staystitch around all edges.

D

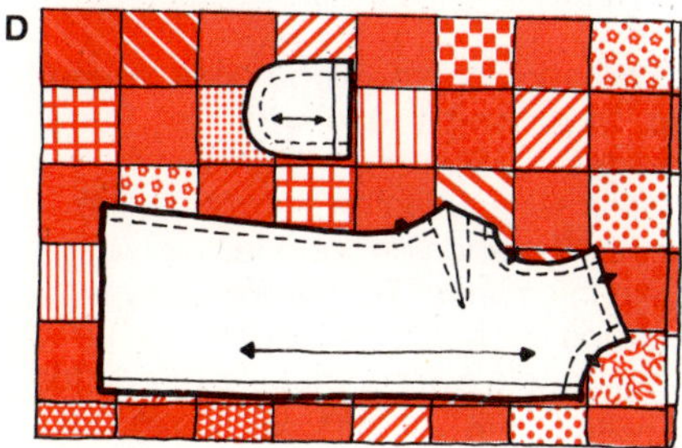

APPLIQUÉ

Fabric pieces of different sizes and shapes placed on a base fabric are called appliqués. Traditional appliqués had their seam allowances turned under; then they were painstakingly sewn to the base fabric with tiny, nearly invisible hand stitches. Today, there are much simpler appliqué methods. Your sewing machine, or your iron and fusible web, will make the job go very fast, indeed.

Designs for appliqué are numerous. Many Simplicity patterns include iron-on transfers for appliqués. You can buy ready-made appliqués, or you can cut around motifs from printed fabrics. To make your own, transfer a favorite design to fabric as described on page 7. Be sure to read Design Decisions, page 5, for more design ideas.

APPLYING

Transfer your design motif to the fabric including 1/4″ (6 mm) seam allowances, and cut out appliqué on the marked line. For multiples of the same motif, follow the method given for cutting patchwork, page 18.

Depending on the effect desired, choose from one of these easy appliqué techniques.

Stitching: Pin the motif to the base fabric and machine-baste 1/4″ (6 mm) from raw edges. Trim close to stitching. Then satin-stitch (close zigzag) all around, covering basting and raw edges (E).

E

Fusing: Intricate motifs may be easily fused in place. Cut identical shapes of fabric and fusible web at the same time, omitting seam allowances. Place the web between the base fabric and the appliqué. Following manufacturer's instructions, fuse in place (A).

If the appliqué fabric has little tendency to ravel, and if the finished project is not going to be subjected to hard use (a wall hanging, for example), there's no need to finish the edges. If it is to be worn or laundered, satin-stitch (close zigzag) around all edges.

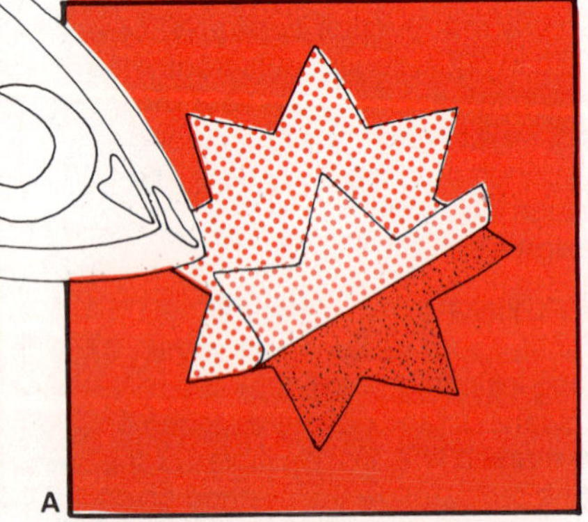

A

Padded Appliqués: For a puffy, three-dimensional look, try this easy method. When cutting appliqués, include ½" (1.3 cm) seam allowances and cut identical pieces of batting (or use a square or circle). Place one or two layers of batting between the appliqué and the base fabric. Baste by machine ½" (1.3 cm) from edge; trim appliqué and batting close to stitching (B). Satin-stitch over the edge.

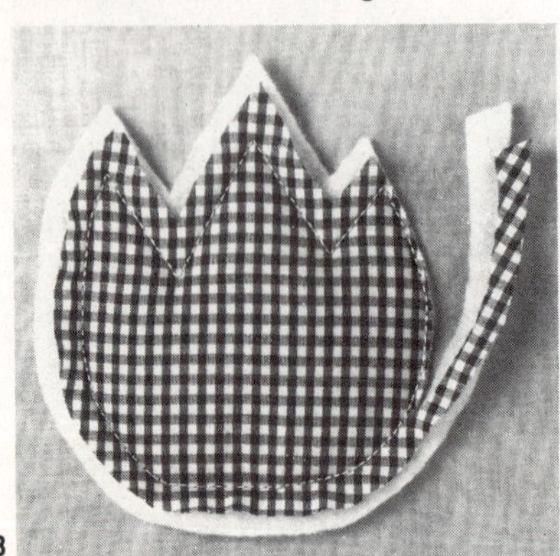

B

QUILTING

This technique, known and used for centuries, produces padded fabrics held together by stitching. The resulting fabric sandwich is warm, durable and decorative all at the same time. It is often the final step in making patchwork or appliqué, whether it's for a large project or small. Quilting can also be used to transform a plain fashion fabric into an interesting, dimensional material with great design potential.

MATERIALS

The fabrics you use should be compatible in weight and texture and should have the same care qualities. If you use cotton or cotton blends for the top, then use the same type of fabric for the backing. Consider using ready-made sheets for top and backing; their size is ideal.

Cotton or polyester batting comes in several standard sheet or bedspread sizes. You can easily cut down or add to batting to get the exact size needed. Either type of batting will wash or dry-clean. If you'd like a very thick, puffy filling, like a comforter, you can stack two or three layers.

Figuring Yardage: For a garment made of quilted fabric, use the yardage chart on the pattern envelope as a guide. Quilting tends to draw up the fabric slightly, thereby reducing the size; it's best to quilt fabric for garment sections first, then cut them out. Or, for a large item like a coverlet, allow an extra inch (2.5 cm) around all edges when planning and cutting. If only part of your project will be quilted, complete the quilted portions before joining them to the other parts. If you are making a fairly large item like a quilt, cut the backing 2" (5 cm) longer and wider than the top to allow for finishing edges (see page 21).

Thread: Use any all-purpose thread, or try quilting thread, which is especially firm and lustrous. Whether you match or contrast the color depends on the effect you'd like to achieve. To make a really strong impact, try polyester buttonhole twist or metallic thread for quilting. Always make a sample first to determine the most pleasing quilting design and thread color, the best tension, pressure and stitch length. To start, loosen tension slightly, lighten pressure and sew 8 stitches per inch (2.5 cm). Then make any necessary adjustments.

SECURING LAYERS

Place the backing fabric wrong side up on a flat surface. Spread the batting, cut or pieced to the same size, over the backing, smoothing it from the center out. Now place the top fabric right side up over the batting, smoothing it in the same way. Pin the layers together. To secure the layers, baste from the center out to each side, diagonally to corners and around edge (C).

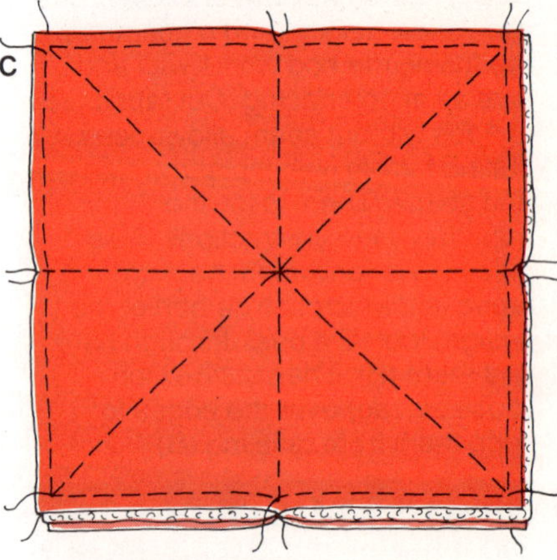

C

QUILTING DESIGNS

Your design choice will depend to some extent on the top fabric. Geometric fabrics lend themselves to square or diamond quilting; free-form motifs suggest outline quilting. Cartridge (channel) and scroll quilting are also attractive (D).

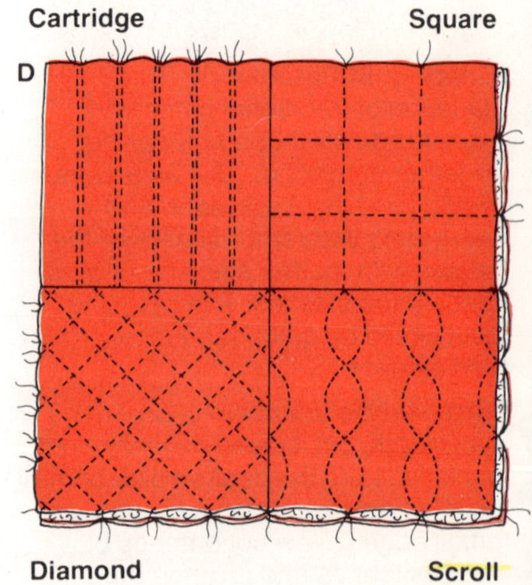

D

The simplest kind of quilting is done in squares or diamonds with the aid of a quilting foot attachment on the machine. Set the guide bar on the quilting foot for the desired spacing between rows, mark the first row of stitching on the fabric, and then stitch. The remaining rows need not be marked since you use the bar to space parallel rows of stitching (A).

A

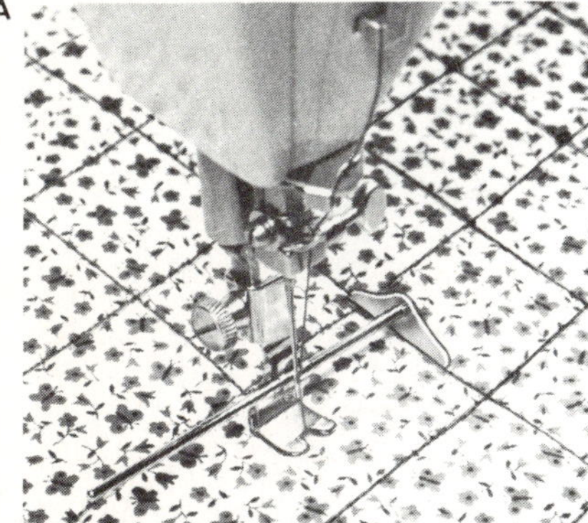

Square Quilting: Mark the center of each edge. With a yardstick and chalk, draw a line connecting the marks at the top and bottom edge and another line connecting the marks at the two side edges to mark the first two rows of quilting. Set the guide bar for the desired spacing between rows—usually 2 to 3″ (5 to 7.6 cm)—and quilt from the center out. Do all the rows in one direction before working in another direction (B).

B

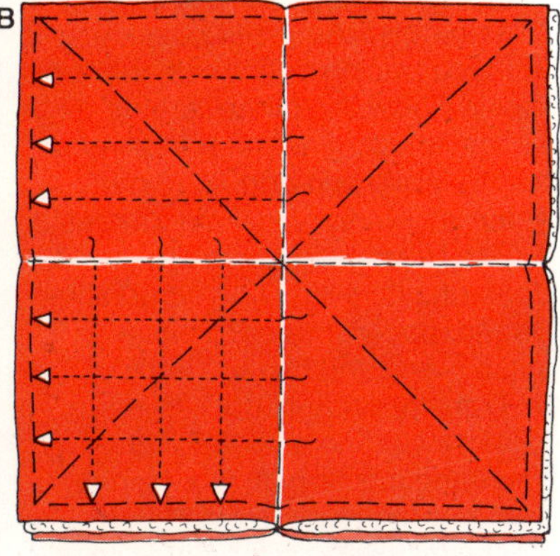

Diamond Quilting: Mark the first two rows by drawing diagonal lines connecting opposite corners, forming an X. Proceed as above.

Cartridge and Scroll: Use the quilting foot guide bar as an aid in cartridge and scroll quilting, too. Just mark your first row and let the bar space the succeeding rows.

C

Outline Quilting: To do outline quilting around a simple motif, first hand-baste along the lines that you intend to quilt. Try to keep most stitching lines 2 to 3″ (5 to 7.6 cm) apart in order to preserve the puffiness of the quilting. Use the quilting foot without guide bar (C).

Tufting: Here is a way of assembling layers that by-passes the sewing machine altogether. Although normally used on a comforter, with tufts at 6 to 8″ (15 to 20.5 cm) intervals, there's no reason why you couldn't adapt this technique to 2 to 3″ (5 to 7.6 cm) intervals for smaller areas on a garment or pillow, for example. Mark the top fabric with a pencil dot for placement of tufts. Thread a large-eyed needle with a length of contrasting yarn and take two or three small stitches through all thicknesses at each mark, leaving long ends (D). Firmly tie the ends twice. Trim, leaving 1″ (2.5 cm) tufts.

D

SEWING AND FINISHING

If your quilted piece is to be part of a garment or a pillow, you can now proceed to use it in your project. If the edges of a quilted piece are to be finished, as for a coverlet or a wall hanging, the best method is binding with double-fold bias tape. See Binding, page 62.

Quilts: Press the raw edge of the backing under ¼″ (6 mm) and fold it over the top. Pin in place and press. To miter corners, open out pressed edges and fold corner diagonally; trim ¼″ (6mm) from fold (E). Fold corner with backing sides together and stitch (F). Press seam open. Turn backing over the top, pin and stitch close to folded edge (G).

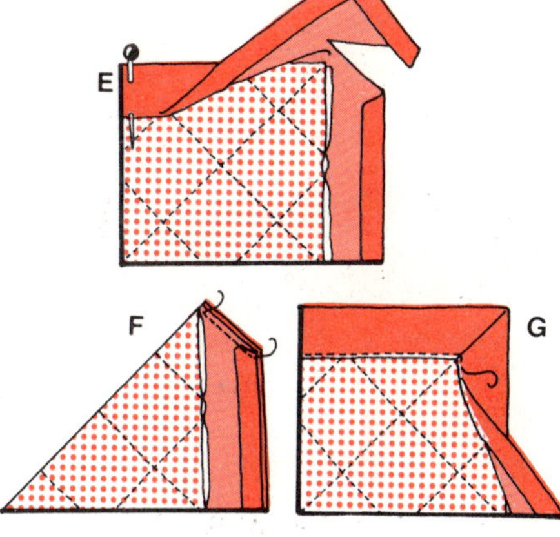

Garments: Since quilteds tend to be bulky, use an unquilted fabric for facings—the one used for the top, or another lightweight, compatible fabric. Or, instead of facings, trim seam allowances away and encase edges in bias tape or braid.

To finish seams, open quilt stitching and trim batting away to stitching line. Then stitch fabric and backing together ⅛″ (3 mm) from edge. Pink or zigzag edge (H). Make buttonholes by machine, or use toggles or frog fasteners.

H

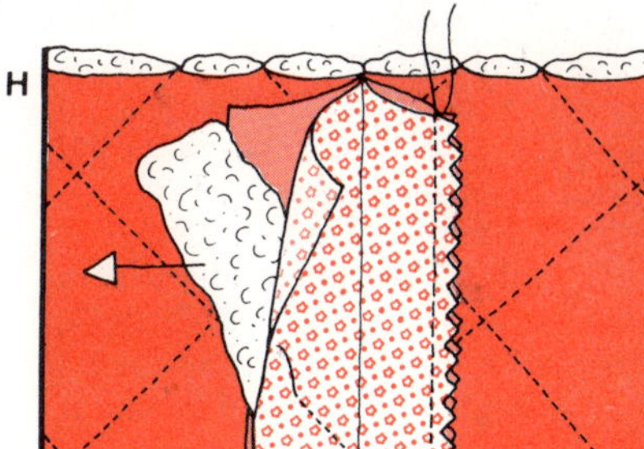

PROJECT INSTRUCTIONS

1/APPLIQUÉD QUILT♥♥♥

Shown on page 14

Materials for finished size 75 x 87" (190.5 x 221 cm): 45" (115 cm) wide cotton fabrics—1⅜ yds. (1.30 m) eggshell, 1¼ yds. (1.15 m) each beige and rust, ¾ yd. (0.70 m) pink; small prints—1⅜ yds. (1.30 m) wine, ⅞ yd. (0.80 m) each rust and eggshell; about 2 yds. (1.85 m) fabric with at least 5 medium-sized floral or other distinct motifs for appliqués; double-bed size sheet for backing; batting for quilt; fusible web; thread to match fabrics.

Directions: (Quilt consists of 4 quarters, 2 as shown and 2 reversed.) **1.** Referring to placement diagram for colors and fabrics, for *each* block shown cut 4 blocks on the crosswise grain as follows: For A, C, E and G, cut rectangles 13 x 15½" (33 x 29.3 cm) and 9 x 11" (23 x 28 cm), and appliqués plus fusible web same size as each piece. Center small rectangle over large one and fuse in place. Fuse appliqué on top, following numbers on diagram for different floral motifs; then satin-stitch around edges of small rectangle and appliqué. For B, D and F, follow same procedure, omitting small rectangle. **2.** Following diagram, assemble quarters with ½" (1.3 cm) seams, using procedure for joining blocks into strips, page 18. Be sure to assemble two of the quarters in reverse by transposing blocks indicated on diagram. **3.** Join completed quarters with ½" (1.3 cm) seams so all G blocks meet in center, and A blocks are at corners. Quilt top is now complete. **4.** Cut batting same size as quilt top; then center top and batting over backing sheet. **5.** Baste layers together; then quilt over seam lines that join blocks (see page 21). **6.** Trim away excess sheet so it is 2" (5 cm) larger all around than top. Using method described for Quilts on page 21, finish the edges.

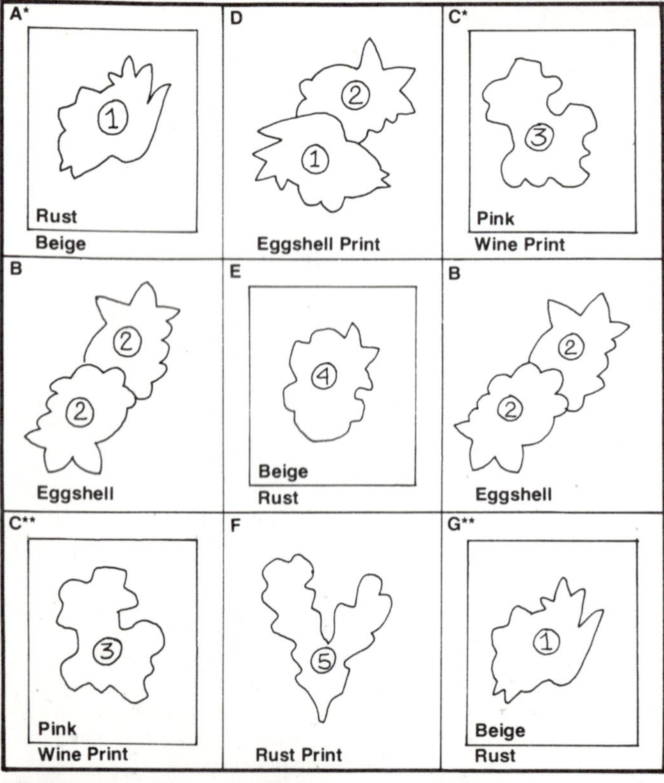

Diagram = ¼ of Quilt

Numbers = different floral motifs

Make 2 in reverse (transpose A* & C*; C & G**)**

2/REVERSIBLE VEST♥♥

Shown on page 15

Simplicity 8065

Materials: Solid fabric for vest, print fabric for lining, thin sheet of polyester batting for quilting, polyester buttonhole twist.

Directions: 1. Cut vest sections from solid, print and batting. Pin batting to wrong side of print sections; baste around edges. **2.** Assemble vest and lining. Baste vest through all layers along main outlines of print (see Outline Quilting, page 21). **3.** Wind bobbin with buttonhole twist. Working on print side, machine-stitch along outlines of print design.

3/APPLIQUÉD OVERALLS♥♥

Shown on pages 2 and 15

Simplicity 7908

Materials: 5" (12.5 cm) squares of five cotton prints; 7" (18 cm) square white cotton fabric; contrasting thread; 1 skein brown six-strand embroidery floss; crewel needle.

Directions: To appliqué, see Stitching, page 19.) **1.** Complete overalls except for attaching pockets. **2.** Enlarge duck and egg designs (opposite) on tracing paper. Place duck tracing over bib, with top of kerchief 2¼" (5.6 cm) below top of bib. Trace around top and sides of bib; trace pocket. Remove tracings after transferring appliqués to fabric or pinning appliqués in position. **3.** Place tracing over beak and feet fabric. Following procedure on page 19 for Applying, transfer beak and feet to fabric and add ¼" (6 mm) seam allowances; cut out shapes. **4.** Use tracing to position feet and beak on bib; pin. Using contrasting thread, apply shapes to bib; also stitch over center line of left foot. **5.** Transfer body of duck to white fabric, including all detail lines. Cut body and position on bib, lapping body slightly over feet and beak. Apply duck; also stitch detail lines. **6.** Trace and cut kerchief; apply to bib. Embroider eye with straight stitches worked close together (see page 46). **7.** Trace egg shape and transfer 2 to each of five print fabrics as on page 19 for Applying. Cut out eggs. **8.** Position 5 eggs on left pocket; pin. Reverse design for right pocket. **9.** Apply eggs. **10.** Stitch pockets to overalls.

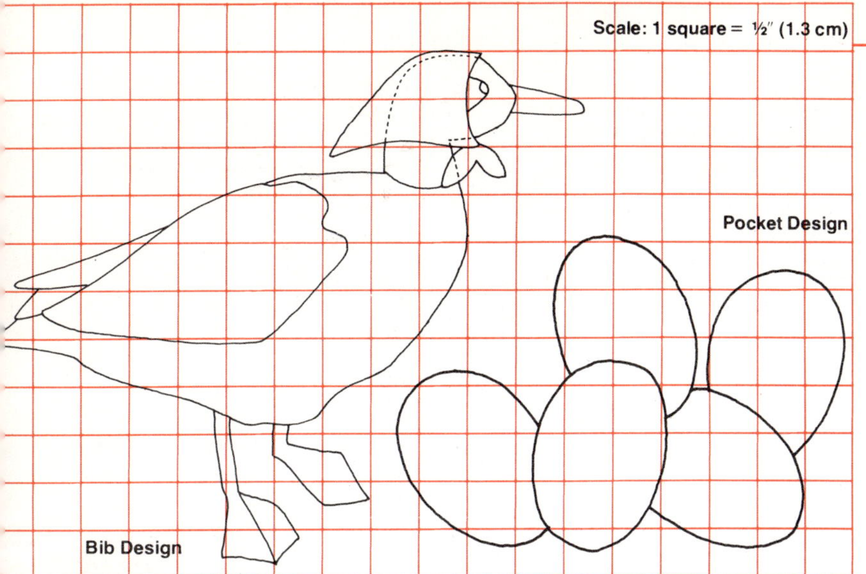

4/HOODED TOP♥

Shown on page 15
Simplicity 8069

Materials (for size 10): 30″ (76 cm) square scarf, or larger, with square border motif.

Directions: 1. Cut out top. **2.** From scarf, cut 2 strips from edge including corners and hemmed edges, 3¼″ (8.2 cm) wide and long enough to fit front opening plus ⅝″ (1.5 cm), and 2 strips along edge, 3¼″ (8.2 cm) wide including hemmed edge and as long as hood edge plus ⅝″ (1.5 cm) seam allowances. At one scarf corner, cut a piece with hemmed edge to cover entire front pocket piece; point of corner should extend 4″ (10 cm) below pocket. From center of scarf, cut 2 triangles 11″ (28 cm) wide at base and 6″ (15 cm) high from point, plus ¼″ (6 mm) seam allowances. Turn under ¼″ (6 mm) on long raw edges of all scarf pieces except pocket. **3.** Sew hood seam. Turn and press hood hem edge to right side. Stitch short raw ends of scarf strips for hood in a ⅝″ (1.5 cm) seam; press open. Right sides together, pin folded strip edge to folded hood edge; edgestitch scarf folds. **4.** Mark front slash; apply facing; press. Pin scarf strips on either side with folded edges even with opening edges and hemmed corners at bottom; strip will extend 3¼″ (8.2 cm) below slash. Edgestitch in place along hemmed scarf edges and along opening. Apply hood and rest of facing. **5.** Pin scarf piece over pocket, positioning point of corner 4″ (10 cm) below pocket. Edgestitch along hemmed edges of scarf. Baste raw edges of scarf to pocket. Trim away scarf point. Apply pocket facing. Edgestitch along opening edges of pocket. Stitch pocket to front. **6.** Press under ¼″ (6 mm) on sides of triangular scarf pieces. Center and pin each to bottom of sleeve, point up. Edgestitch. Complete top.

5/APPLIQUÉD STOLE♥

Shown on page 15
Simplicity 8076 (skirt)

Materials (for stole): 1½ yds. (1.40 m) 54″ (137 cm) wide soft, solid color fabric; extra floral skirt fabric for appliqués; fusible web; thread.

Directions: 1. Trim 4″ (10 cm) along one selvage of stole fabric; then cut in half crosswise to make two pieces 27″ (68.5 cm) wide. Seam two short edges. Narrow-hem long edges. Make 2″ (5 cm) fringe on ends (see page 63). **2.** Cut appliqués from skirt fabric. **3.** Place appliqués with fusible web underneath, at each end of stole as in diagram, overlapping slightly. **4.** Pin, fuse, and satin-stitch.

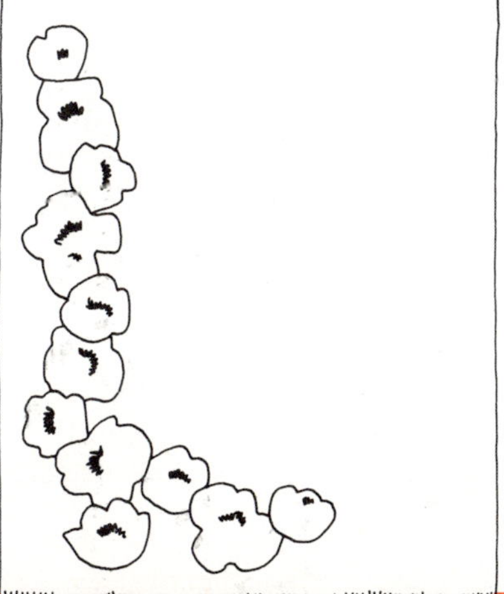

6/APPLIQUÉD APRON♥♥

Shown on page 16
Simplicity 7254

Materials: ⅛ yard (0.15 m) each cotton print, stripe, check and solid; fusible web; thread.

Directions: 1. Complete apron. **2.** Make templates for triangle and square (see page 7). Cut 4 squares of solid, 16 triangles of each print and fusible web the same size. **3.** With fusible web under each piece, center one square 5″ (12.5 cm) above hemline and place triangles around it for 8-pointed star motif (see page 16). Place one motif on either side and one above first, points touching. **4.** Pin, fuse and satin-stitch.

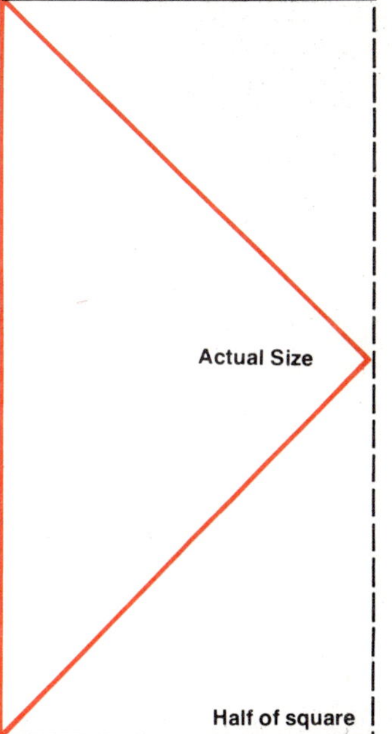

7/HOUSE PILLOW♥♥

Shown on page 16
Simplicity 7734

Materials: Two pieces of cotton prints 6 x 13″ (15 x 33 cm), scraps of five different prints (two green), scraps of three solids, 8″ (20.5 cm) piece of ¼″ (6 mm) wide ribbon, 6″ (15 cm) piece of ¼″ (6 mm) scalloped edging, 2″ (5 cm) of middy braid, 22″ (56 cm) of white twill tape, thread, fusible web.

Directions: 1. Assemble pillow up to step C. **2.** Enlarge diagram (page 24) and trace twice; number pieces. Use one tracing to cut fabric shapes and fusible strips as follows: # 1 and 2—large print pieces; #3 and

Scale: 1 square = 1″ (2.5 cm)

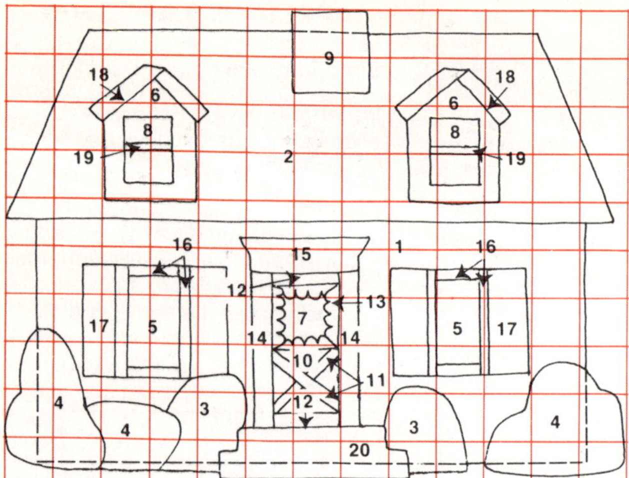

4—green prints; #5, 6, 9 and 20—different prints; #10, 14 and 15—same color solid; #7, 8 and 17—different solids; #11, 12, and 16—twill tape; #13—edging; #18—ribbon; #19—middy braid. **3.** Pin uncut tracing over pillow as a guide for placing pieces; remove for fusing. After pieces are fused, satin-stitch around all edges. Position and fuse all pieces as follows: #1; #2 overlapping #1; #3-10; crisscross #11 pieces; butt #12-15, and #16 and 17; #18, forming fold at top; center #19 over #8; #20. **4.** Complete pillow.

8/PATCHWORK NECKTIE♥

Shown on page 16
Simplicity 7701

Materials: 1/8 yd. (0.15 m) each of five 54″ (137 cm) wide wool plaids.

Directions: 1. Cut 23 blocks 3 x 8″ (7.6 x 20.5 cm). Alternating plaids, stitch two blocks together at short ends in a 1/4″ (6 mm) seam; press open. Repeat 5 more times. **2.** Tape pattern pieces C and D together at seam line, overlapping seam allowances. **3.** Arrange pattern over blocks, with double-patch blocks at bottom front of tie. Place seam line of first bottom strip 1 1/2″ (3.8 cm) from tie fold line and raw edge along cutting line. For remaining blocks, place seam line approximately 2 1/4″ (5.6 cm) away from previous seam line, overlapping 1/4″ (6 mm). Continue with single blocks under pattern, making sure blocks extend to cutting line (see diagram). Pin and stitch blocks in 1/4″ (6 mm) seams and press open. **4.** Cut and complete tie.

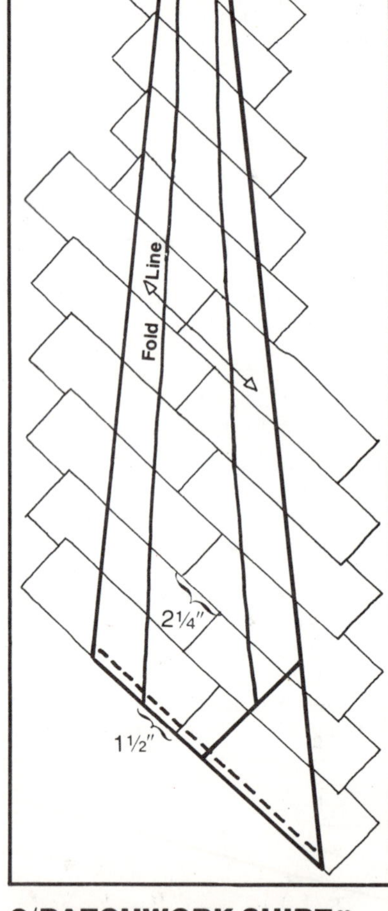

9/PATCHWORK SHIRT♥

Shown on page 16
Simplicity 7051, View 1

Materials for contrast: 4 cotton prints—see page 18 for figuring yardage; fusible web; thread.

Directions: 1. Cut out shirt. **2.** Follow method for Super-Quick Patchwork shown on page 19, to make staggered patchwork from prints. Fuse to yoke and cuffs. Trim away excess patchwork. Zigzag-stitch over patchwork edges. **3.** Cut two triangles 3 1/8″ (7.9 cm) high from base to point to fit collar point. Fuse triangles to interfaced collar. Zigzag-stitch over horizontal edge. **4.** Assemble shirt. **5.** Using a decorative stitch and contrasting thread, stitch 1/4″ (6 mm) from edge of yoke, collar and cuffs, and along topstitching lines of front bands.

10/PATCHWORK TOTE♥♥

Shown on page 16
Simplicity 7515, View 2

Materials: 5 different velveteens and corduroys—see pattern and page 18 for figuring yardage.

Directions: 1. Cut and seam patches in staggered patchwork method (see Shortcut Seaming, page 18) to form patchwork of 3″ (7.6 cm) squares. Reserve one 3 1/2 x 25″ (9 x 63.5 cm) piece of corduroy for facing. **2.** Cut bag and handle pieces from patchwork. Cut facing from reserved piece of corduroy. **3.** Assemble bag.

11/APPLIQUÉD ENVELOPE♥

Shown on page 16
Simplicity 7004, View 2

Materials: Fabric for bag and lining; for appliqués—5 x 6″ (12.5 x 15 cm) pieces of dark and light fabric; thread; batting in same amount as bag plus 1/4 yd. (0.25 m).

Directions: 1. Cut bag, batting and lining. Sandwich batting between and baste. Using quilting foot, quilt with lengthwise rows 1″ (2.5 cm) apart. **2.** Assemble bag; bind edges. **3.** Enlarge appliqué patterns, adding 1/2″ seam allowances, transfer to fabric and cut 1 dark and 2 light pieces plus batting. **4.** Apply to flap (see Padded Appliqués, page 20). Sew snap.

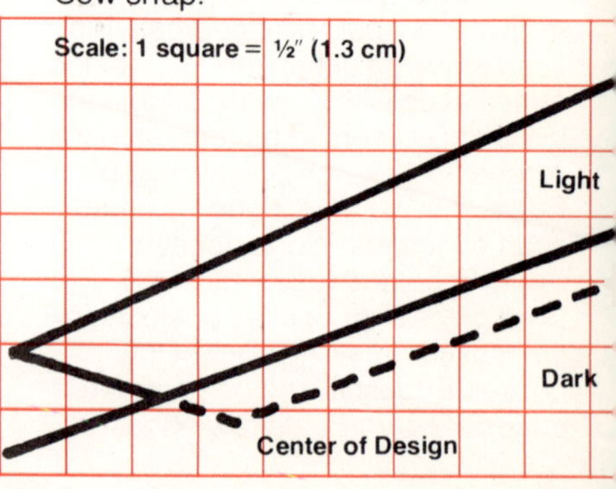

IDEA FILE

Contemporary patchwork, appliqué and quilting open up a whole new world of creative sewing. Our quick machine methods cut down on the time needed for each project. Here, more inspirational ideas.

Patches à la crazy-quilt style are fused to a pretty background fabric for a unique pillow.♥♥

Nifty popover top is given a one-of-a-kind look with diamond quilting on yoke. Quick to make, fabric is machine-quilted before cutting.♥♥

How does your garden grow? With tulips in a row! These, machine-appliquéd, have tie stems to close this Jiffy® jacket.♥

Stitching rickrack on with channel quilting is a nice way to highlight every row distinctively.♥♥

Bright maxi-blocks make a new patchwork vest. Add seams at pattern topstitching lines, cut patches, then machine-quilt.♥♥

Quilted cases are handy for stashing goodies like hosiery or sewing things. Machine-stitched appliqués identify your treasures in a flash! ♥

FABULOUS FABRICS

THE ETHNIC TOUCH

Good News! Today's fashion fabrics come with inspiration already built-in. With a little planning, stunning prints, rich textures and stylish fakes practically sew themselves into the most admired looks. Create your own folkloric fantasies with the wealth of fabrics at your fingertips.

12 Bold felt cutouts, inspired by a Navajo wall-hanging, add a great deal of design interest to this fantastic vest. The cutouts are easily glued in place, and there are no raw edges to finish! ♥♥

13 Do-it-yourself print mixing combines small floral prints in tiers of ruffles to give this draw-string skirt a super, sassy look. ♥♥

14 The beguiling look of peasantry in this three-piece ensemble is pulled together artfully, but simply, with the help of these three coordinating floral prints. ♥

Instructions, pages 35-36

7931
7862
7880

FABULOUS FABRICS

Creative use of fabric goes outdoors in rich, rugged textures of pseudo-suede and crunchy wool tweed. They're impressive all by themselves, but they take kindly to mixing as well. Just take a look at these two beauties.

15 His patchwork yoke shows off a beautiful mix of masculine textures—tweeds, plaids and plush corduroy—in a coordinated color scheme.♥

16 There's nothing like the look of suede for the great outdoors. And, there's no need to pamper this super fake—just hole-punch a sporty design and lace strips 'round the edges.♥♥♥

Complete how-to's on page 36

THOSE FABULOUS FABRICS

Make the most of your fabric for an easy way to Sew Something Special. There's no need to add extras. Just take creative advantage of what's available—such as border or scarf prints, fake leathers and suedes, all sorts of textures and prints, even sheeting by the yard and towels! Use special layouts to make the most of large scale and border prints. Make interesting fabric mixtures of color, scale, print or texture. And, have fun with new methods developed for non-ravel fabrics. None of the techniques are hard and many will amaze you with their exciting results. Here's all the know-how you'll need to turn your fabric fantasies into truly fabulous fashions!

SPECIAL LAYOUTS

Large scale, border or scarf prints require careful planning and layout for best use of the design. Lace, eyelet borders, sheets, and towels need special layouts, too. Once you plan your design, you'll see how simple they are to sew.

BUYING ADVICE

Because of the decorative nature of these fabrics, you'll want to make them the main focus of your garment. Choose a pattern style that will play up the print—one with few seams, pieces or details to compete with your fabric. Jiffy® or Simple-to-Sew™ patterns and those with drawstring waistlines or no waist seams are good choices (A). Or, use a pattern which shows the type of print you are using and includes special layouts and yardage requirements.

If you choose a pattern not shown in the type of print you've chosen, check the pattern pieces on the envelope back. Pattern edges where a border will be placed must be on the straight grain or should be straightened (B). Use only patterns with slightly curved edges or you may distort the style when straightening the edge. If you're planning to match a design at the seams, make sure the seam edges are either straight or only on a slight angle to make matching easier. Remember to buy an extra ½ to 1 yard (.50 to .95 m) of fabric or two or three extra repeats of the print so you'll have enough to plan your design placement. If the fabric is expensive, lay the main pattern pieces on it in the store to determine the exact yardage you'll need. To be sure of the correct design placement on your finished garment, make all your pattern adjustments before laying out and cutting the pattern pieces.

BORDER PRINTS

Borders are edgings designed right into fabrics. Although they're naturals for hemlines, there are other clever ways to sew with border prints.

Horizontal Borders: For hemlines and other horizontal uses of borders, follow these suggestions:

- Decide on finished garment length; then position hemline on border edge where it looks best.
- Lay out pattern pieces on the crosswise grain. First position pieces that use the border—front, then back and other pieces with border; center dominant motifs. Match borders at side seams where possible. Place remaining pieces where they look best, on or above the border (B).

A

B

Creative Ideas: Use a lacy border to ruffle up the top edge of a camisole or peasant blouse. Ruffles cut on straight grain are perfect places for borders (A). Circle a hemline with a border (B). Accent a pocket top, cuff or sleeve with a border (B). Top a sundress bodice or the edges of kimono sleeves with a border. Locate the border to focus on your best feature—near the hem for good legs or at the top to make narrow shoulders appear wider. Brighten curtains or draperies—border them!

Vertical Borders: Vertical borders work best on pattern pieces with straight vertical seams or edges on the straight grain (C), unless the border is used for small details.

- When placing a border along a front opening, match the border motif at front seam lines (D).
- Lay all pattern pieces on the straight, lengthwise grain. Place pieces that use the border first (E).
- Position the main motif carefully to avoid breaking up its design.
- Place remaining pieces on straight grain, beyond the border (E).

Creative Ideas: Play up side detailing; border the side seams of a tunic or the edge of a tabard. Make a wrap skirt with a border along the wrapped edge (C). Highlight the front edges of a vest.

Use borders as trims on home furnishings. Cut the border off the fabric, allowing ¼″ (6 mm) extra on both edges. Press raw edges under and stitch the border to pillows, tablecloths, bedspreads, curtains or placemats, mitering corners as for Wide Trims, page 62.

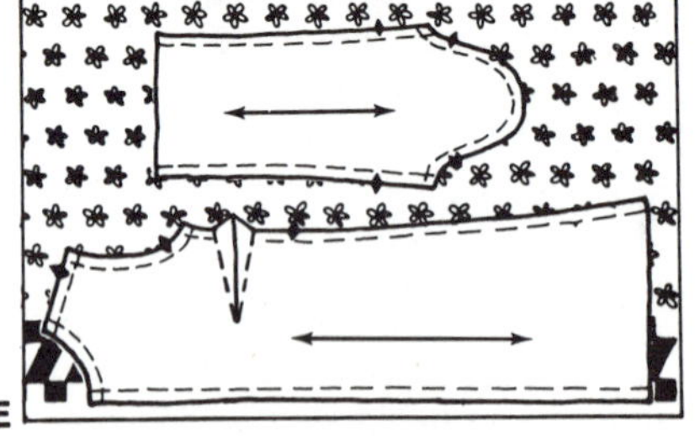

LARGE SCALE PRINTS

Bold designs can have a big fashion impact. Whether they are florals, geometrics or scarf prints, the large scale prints make striking garments, accessories or home furnishings.

There are two ways of handling a large scale or scarf print. You can treat the fabric as you would an allover print (if the motifs or squares are not too large—6″ (15 cm) square or smaller); or center a main motif or square to make the design the main focus of attention.

Layout Advice: For large print placement, use these suggestions:

- Determine finished length of garment before placing hemline along border edges of a large scarf print or below a large motif.
- Position major pieces such as front, back and sleeves first.
- Try not to cut into a large motif or break it up during layout (F, G).
- Center large squares or motifs, placing them at center front and back (G) or position a square on either side of the center front seam or the opening (see A opposite).
- Match the design at side seams where possible.
- Small pieces—facings, collars, cuffs, and pockets—can be placed within a scarf print border, or beyond main motif (see A opposite).
- Avoid placing large motifs over bust or hip areas; the print will not only be distorted, but will also make the body appear larger at these points.

Creative Ideas: Small fashion items—bathing suits, halter tops and shorts—are perfect for using scarves or large prints dramatically.

How about custom accessories for your home . . . decorator pillows made from two large scarves or other maxi-prints, or a bedspread with a large print centered and quilted?

SHEETS AND TOWELS

Today, brightly designed fabrics are often found in linen and domestics departments. Since designer sheets and towels have become such pacesetters in color and design, they have zoomed out of the linen closet right into many fashion wardrobes!

Pre-hemmed items have some advantages over fabrics by the yard. Their width makes it possible to skip some of the seams required by normal-width fabrics. The hemmed edges are helpful for curtains and other home decorating items. Towels also have the bonus of finished edges, woven borders or fringe that can be used at garment edges.

Most sheets, curtains or tablecloths are permanent-press; they're ideal for easy-care garments, and they're money-savers, too! A twin sheet contains over 5 yards (4.60 m) of fabric, making the cost per yard (m) very low. To use borders of sheets and towels, follow directions for Special Layouts, pages 29-30.

Creative Ideas: Be imaginative with sheets and towels! Stitch up a Jiffy® playsuit from a patterned towel (B). Sew an easy caftan from a boldly printed sheet (C). Make a tablecloth and napkins from a printed sheet—it's a real money-saver! Use lace curtains or tablecloth and napkins for a beach coverup or luxurious evening ensemble. Use the nubby, natural texture of dish towels for contrast yokes, pockets, collars and tops to contrast with smoother textures.

FABRIC MIXING

Mix two or more fabrics in a garment to make a strong fabric statement. Combine color, texture, scale or print direction to create a rich, interesting fashion mixture.

BUYING ADVICE

Consider your options. Mix fabrics by cutting the body of a garment in one fabric and the details in another; or, appliqué one fabric over another.

If your pattern does not include yardage requirements for mixing fabrics, adjust the amount for your design plan. Combine fabrics that have the same care qualities and similar weight. Coordinated fabrics that are designed to go together make mixing a snap! See pages 27 and 37 for more ideas.

A

Accessories and home furnishings are ideal for fabric mixing. A collage of fabrics—one for the main part, others for a border, appliqué or details—makes an unusual wall hanging or bedspread.

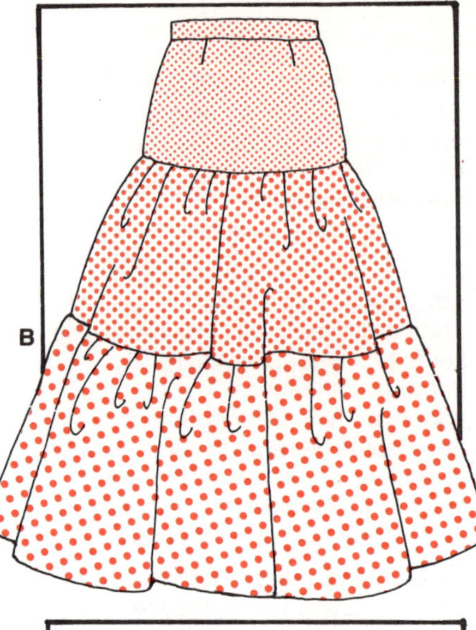

B

C

D

MIXING HINTS

Texture: Combine textures, keeping color, design or scale alike—soft voile and crisp ciré; ribbed corduroy and smooth velveteen; napped pseudo-suede and sleek poplin; shiny satin and matte crepe.

Design: Change motifs, keeping texture, color or scale constant—a stripe with a check or dot (A); a medium-size floral with a tiny pinstripe or check; tweed with herringbone, check or plaid (as shown in our man's jacket, page 28).

Scale: Vary scale, keeping design, color or texture the same—try mixing large and small checks, stripes, plaids or dots (B); large and small geometrics of the same design; a bold floral with a smaller one (see how we mixed prints in our peasant outfit, page 27).

Color: Mix colors, keeping texture, design or scale constant—a print with a solid that picks up a dominant color; the same print with the colors reversed, positive/negative (C); multi-color prints of the same scale and type, like small florals (see ruffled skirt, page 27).

Direction: Create a mix from a single fabric by laying out your pattern so the design changes direction—stripes on the bias for chevrons; vertical and horizontal, or vertical and bias contrast (D); plaid details on the bias are always effective, as on yokes, pockets, collars and cuffs.

To change a straight grainline to bias (you can do this on small detail areas without distorting the garment), fold pattern piece crosswise at center of grainline. Bring folded edge to original grainline and crease. Open out. Draw a line along one diagonal crease for the new bias grainline (E).

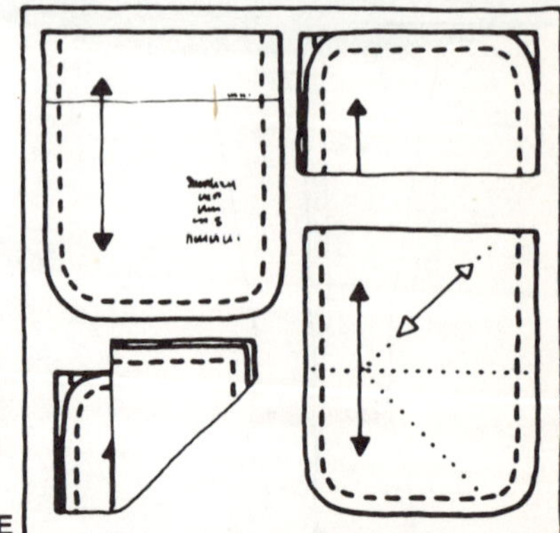

E

PSEUDO-SUEDES AND NON-RAVEL FABRICS

Modern technology has produced new fabrics that offer many creative possibilities. Leather and suede have been supplemented with easy-care synthetic look-alikes. Other fabrics—vinyl, melton, felt and blanket fabrics—can be handled in a similar way, too. Since these fabrics won't fray, creative edge and hem treatments are easy to do.

GENERAL HINTS

Before you buy your pattern and lay it out, read these tips:

• Use only non-ravel fabrics for the techniques that follow. If the fabric is napped, use the "with nap" layout.

• Choose a simple pattern with little easing and few darts. Avoid pleats and fullness as non-ravel fabrics are often too bulky to gather or drape well. Make pattern adjustments now or use a pattern that's already fitted since needle holes are often permanent on synthetic suedes and leathers.

• For marking fake leather, use a smooth-edge tracing wheel and dressmaker's carbon on the wrong side, and pins for ends of darts or button placement. Mark fake suede with a smooth-edge tracing wheel. Mark melton and blanket fabrics with pins and a chalk pencil.

SEAMS

Instead of pins, which leave marks on vinyls and suede-likes, hold layers together for stitching with paper clips or double-faced tape. Use sharp wedge-pointed needles for stitching; the needle size may range from 11 to 16, depending on the weight of the fabric. For durability, use 8 to 10 stitches per inch (2.5 cm), and use strong thread—silk, polyester, cotton-covered polyester or heavy-duty mercerized.

Use shortcut techniques to achieve a professional look, and do creative seam and edge treatments. While you can use conventional seams on most non-ravel fabrics, seam allowances on vinyl and fake suede must be flattened by gluing with rubber cement and pounding, or by topstitching. Felt, melton and blanket fabrics are often topstitched, too. So a lapped seam will often give the best results on all.

Lapped Seams: For a smooth, professional look, trim away seam allowance of lapped section (A); tape-mark seam line on other section (B). Lap trimmed piece over untrimmed one. Fuse (except vinyl), tape or glue (C). Stitch 1/8″ (3 mm) away from edge and again 1/4″ (6 mm) away from first stitching (D).

Decorative Seams: On a Lapped Seam, use double zigzag instead of straight stitching. Or pink the edge of the overlap and double-stitch as for lapped seams above. Try stitching with contrasting thread for a sporty look.

COLLARS

Collars can be attached by the Lapped Seam method, if neck edges have facings. Assemble and trim garment and facing as for Lapped Seam. Trim 5/8″ (1.5 cm) from outside edges of collar pieces (not collar neck edges). Staystitch and clip neckline curves on collar pieces. Lap neck facing over one collar neck edge to seam line; tape or glue (do not fuse). Edgestitch facing to collar (E). Repeat for garment neck edge with other collar piece. Glue collar sections together along neck seam line. Fuse, tape or glue outer edges of all layers together. Double-stitch garment and collar edges from bottom of garment up (F).

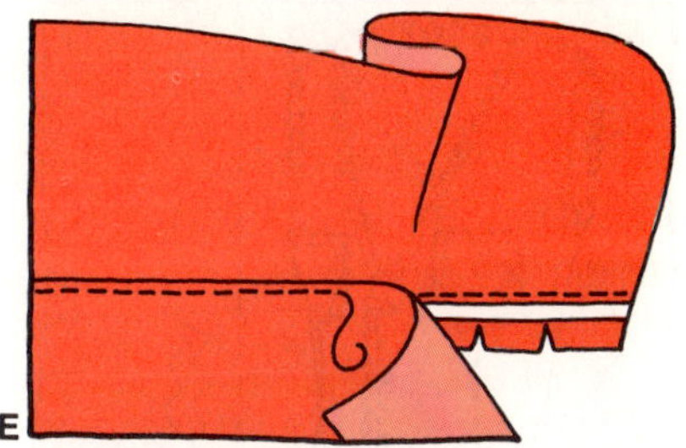

E

F

EDGES

Edges on non-ravel fabrics can be finished in a variety of ways. Due to the body of these fabrics, most interfacings and facings can be omitted. When a facing is necessary for firmness (as on a cuff, collar, or jacket front edge), apply the facing using the flat method.

Flat-Faced Edge: Assemble garment and facings separately. Trim 5/8″ (1.5 cm) from outside edges. Fuse, tape or glue facing to garment, wrong sides together; double-stitch edges; see Lapped Seams (G).

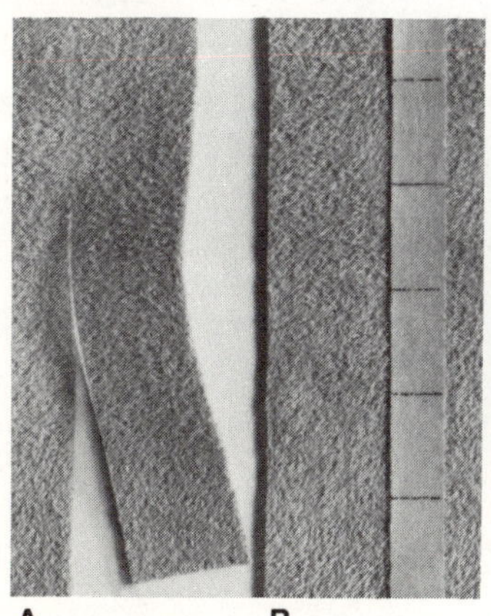

A B

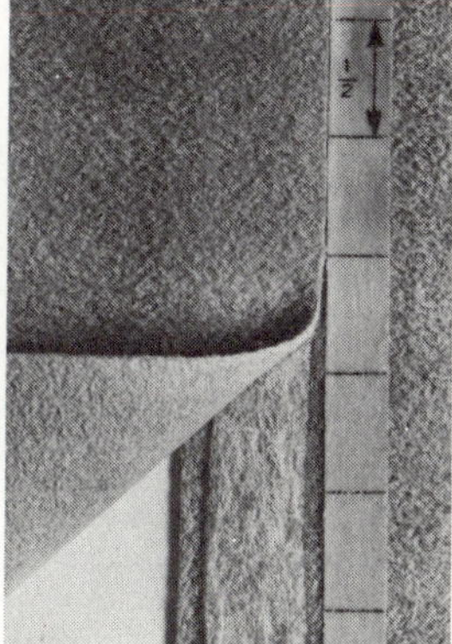

C

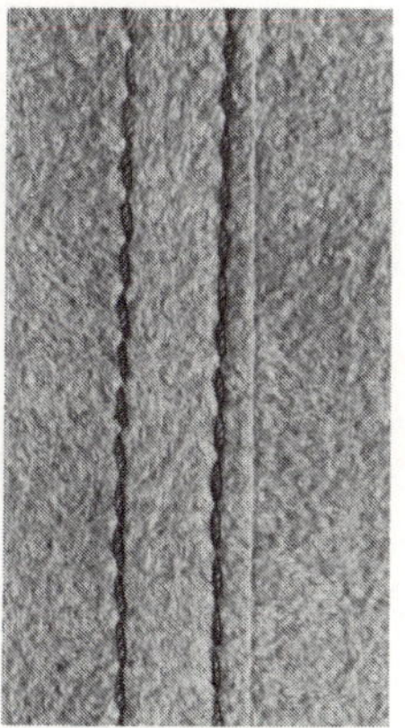

D

G

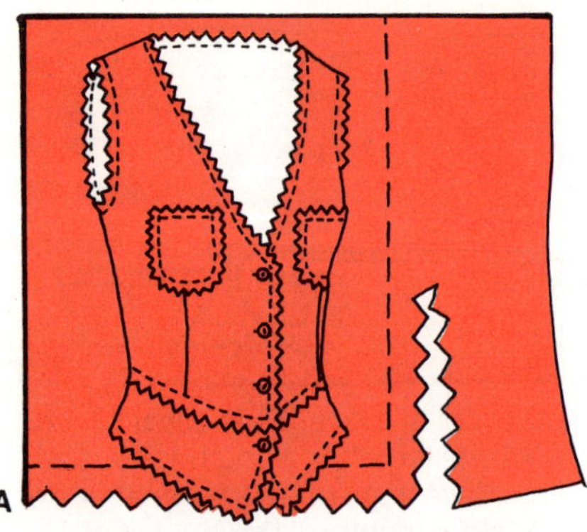

A

Unfaced Edges: On fabrics with enough body to omit facings, turn edge under and double-stitch as for Lapped Seams, or double zigzag-stitch. Or, trim edge away and topstitch; or pink and stitch (A). On felt, melton and blankets, trim away seam allowance and satin-stitch (close zigzag) over edge (B).

B

BUTTONHOLES

For felt, melton and blanket fabrics, interface fabric and stitch a regular buttonhole by machine. On vinyls and mock leathers or suedes, use a straight-stitched buttonhole; a regular buttonhole would split these fabrics.

To make straight-stitched buttonholes, stitch a rectangle around buttonhole marking twice, two or three stitches wide and buttonhole length. Use 12 to 15 stitches per inch (2.5 cm). Mark ends of buttonhole with pins; slash with a single-edge razor blade (C).

C

CREATIVE IDEAS

Decorative edge treatments and appliqués are so easy to do when there's no fraying or raveling.

Lacing: Lacings on a garment create decorative closures, seams or edges. To lace a closure edge, you'll need to sew on hooks, apply eyelets, or make loops. Measure and mark eyelet or hook placement first. To

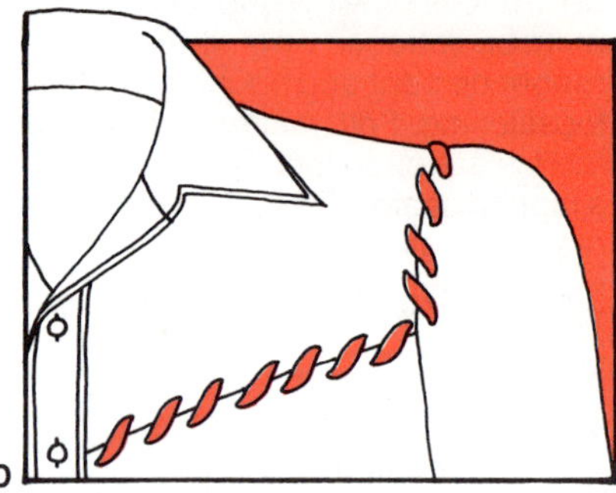

D

lace along a seam, mark locations for ⅛″ (3 mm) slits on either side of seam or along an edge. Slits should be ¼″ to ⅜″ (6 mm to 1 cm) from seam or edge. Lace with leather strips (D), macramé cord, yarns or ribbon (see psuedo-suede jacket, page 28).

Punching: Decorate a garment by punching small holes to form a design (E). A rotary leather punch (available at craft and leather shops) with spokes for punching different size holes will punch through any

E

thickness of leather or synthetic. Or use an eyelet punch. Test your design first on a scrap of fabric, then mark design with pins or a pencil and punch the actual garment. If you plan to do lacing along a punched edge, face the edge and punch ¼″ to ⅜″ (6 mm to 1 cm) from edge.

Scallops: You can cut scallops or other designs along edges (E). With a ruler and pencil, mark the points of the scallops, spacing them evenly. Draw the curves with the help of a spool of thread; then cut.

Fringe: Cut fringe along edge of garment. On the wrong side of your fabric, draw a straight line parallel to the edge to be fringed and as far away from the edge as the fringe is deep—from 1″ to 3″ (2.5 to 7.5 cm). Mark off width of fringe at ¼″ (6 mm) intervals. Then cut fringe from the edge to marked line (F).

F

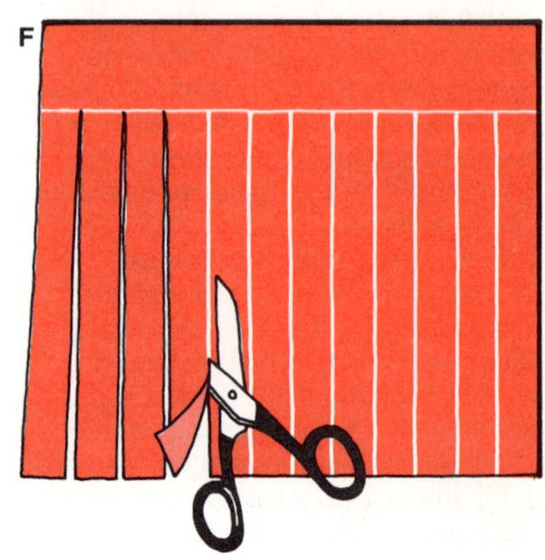

PROJECT INSTRUCTIONS

12/NAVAJO VEST♥♥

Shown on page 26
Simplicity 7614

Materials: ⅛ yd. (.15 m) each of 72″ (183 cm) wide beige and brown felt, 8″ (20.5 cm) square of rust felt, brown thread, tracing paper, lightweight cardboard, pinking shears, fabric glue, paper plate, flat wood stick or toothpick for applying glue.

Directions: 1. Complete vest, using double-stitched, flat faced edge methods on page 33. **2.** Trace entire basic design unit. Trace one of each shape separately to make cutting patterns of lightweight cardboard (see Multiple Transfer, page 7). Use cardboard patterns to outline half the number of shapes in colors needed, following chart at right. With pinking shears, cut out shapes through two layers of felt pinned together. Keep separate shapes grouped together. **3.** Place vest on flat surface with fronts face up. Place shapes (turned over so markings don't show) on vest, following basic design unit and color guide. Start at lower right side, with point of beige chevron just touching inner row of topstitching at bottom of vest. Check alignment of each basic unit by placing tracing on top. Position three more units on right half of vest, with ½″ (1.3 cm) between design units. Position designs on left side in same manner. **4.** Squeeze some glue onto paper plate. Beginning at lower edge, pick up one shape at a time and, using stick or toothpick, apply glue to back. Replace on vest, pressing down to adhere. Repeat this procedure until all the shapes have been applied. **5.** Tassels: Cut eight 1½″ (3.8 cm) squares of brown felt. Make close parallel cuts from one edge to within ½″ (1.3 cm) of opposite edge. Wrap a tassel around each tie and secure by taking several stitches with a double strand of brown thread through all layers of felt.

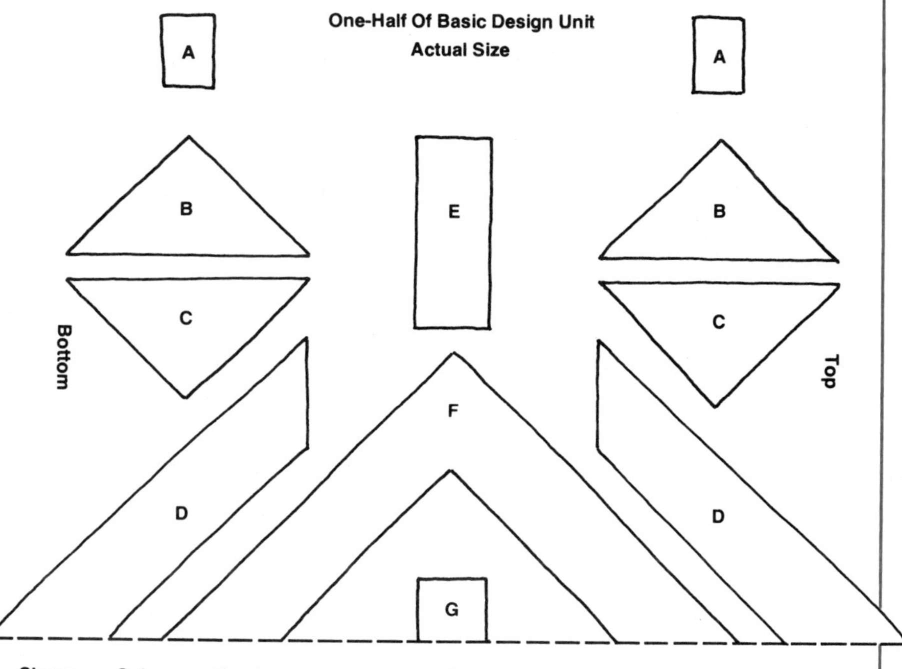

Shape	Color	Number
A	beige	32
B	brown	32
C	rust	32
D	beige	16
E	beige	16
F	brown	8
G	rust	8

13/SKIRT WITH RUFFLE TIERS♥♥

Shown on page 27
Simplicity 7862

Materials: ¾ yd. (0.70 m) each of five small prints (one same as skirt), each 45″ (115 cm) wide (ruffle fabrics must be of same weight as the skirt fabric).

Directions: 1. Complete skirt. **2.** For ruffles, cut strips 5″ (12.5 cm) wide on cross grain of each fabric. Piece strips where necessary with ¼″ (6 mm) seams to make 6 yd. (5.50 m) lengths for each ruffle. Join ends of each strip. To hem strips, turn and press one edge under ¼″ (6 mm) twice; machine-stitch. **3.** To gather bottom ruffle, make two rows of long machine stitches, ¼″ (6 mm) apart, the first one ½″ (1.3 cm) from raw edge. **4.** Pin ruffle to skirt, wrong side to right side, with raw edge of ruffle 2″ (5 cm) from bottom of skirt. Pull up bobbin thread to gather ruffle to fit skirt. Stitch close to gathering stitches; do not press ruffle. Repeat for next three ruffles, placing raw edges 2½″ (6.3 cm) apart. **5.** For top ruffle, turn under ⅞″ (2.2 cm) at top of last strip; press. Make two rows of long machine stitching ½″ (1.3 cm) from top of fold and gather to fit around skirt 2½″ (6.3 cm) above raw edge of last ruffle. Pin wrong side of ruffle to right side of skirt. Stitch along gathering stitches, forming a ½″ (1.3 cm) heading at top of the ruffle.

14/PEASANT OUTFIT♥

Shown on page 27
Simplicity 7880

Materials: 3 coordinating prints in different scales—yardage as on pattern except where noted. For blouse, use medium size print; for yoke, collar and bias strips, use small print—1 yard (0.95 m) of 45″ (115 cm) fabric; for shirt, use striped print; for vest, use corduroy in color to match background of blouse.

Directions: 1. Cut blouse and contrast yoke and collar according to View 1 layouts. Extra fabric from yoke and collar will be used to bind vest. Cut skirt with stripes running horizontally. **2.** Assemble blouse and skirt. Assemble vest, substituting bias strips of yoke fabric 2″ (5 cm) wide for foldover braid. Cut enough to go around armholes, front, neck and bottom edges, piecing where necessary. To piece bias strips, lap

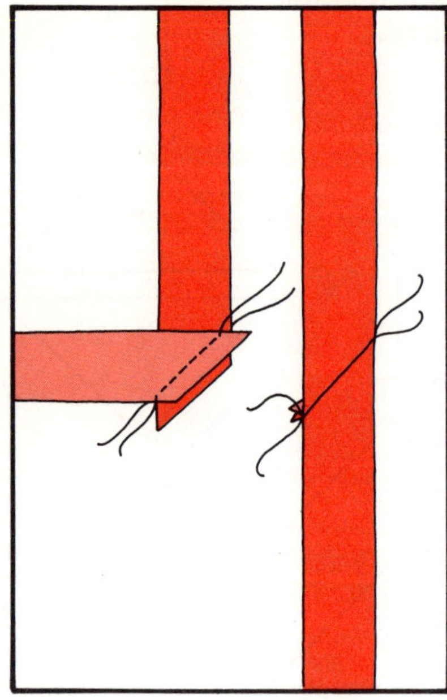

ends with right sides together, so strips are at right angles to each other; stitch on straight grain in a ¼″ (6 mm) seam, starting and ending at point where strips cross; press open. Trim away extending points. **3.** To apply bias binding, turn ¼″ (6 mm) under on one long edge of strip; press. Pin unpressed edge of strip to vest, right sides together, easing strip around curves. Stitch in a ½″ (1.3 mm) seam. Fold strip over edge of vest, pin pressed edge of strip to inside and machine-stitch along binding seam from right side, catching binding underneath.

15/SHIRT-JACKET ♥

Shown on page 28
Simplicity 7698

Materials (for patchwork yoke): remnants of wool tweeds and plaids and corduroy, coordinated color thread, fusible web.

Directions: 1. Lap yoke pattern over back pattern, matching seam lines; pin together. Use this combined pattern to cut out back in one piece. Cut out other jacket pieces. **2.** Place back section right side up on flat surface. From seam line at center back of neck, measure down 8½″ (21.8 cm). With chalk, draw a line straight across back through mark; area above line will be patched. **3.** Cut remnants into squares and rectangles varying in size from about 1½″ (3.8 cm) to 5″ (12.5 cm), cutting identical pieces of fusible web at same time. Pin web to back of each patch. **4.** Beginning at chalk line, arrange patches to cover entire area above line, letting patches overlap as desired. When final arrangement has been determined, pin each patch to back section. Trim away excess patchwork at armhole, neck and shoulder edges. Fuse patches in place. **5.** Satin-stitch around edges of each patch. **6.** Complete jacket.

16/PUNCHED AND LACED JACKET♥♥♥

Shown on page 28
Simplicity 7786

Materials: Non-ravel fabric for jacket plus ⅛ yd. (0.15 m) for strips, adjustable hole puncher, tapestry needle, fabric glue, tracing paper.

Directions: 1. Complete jacket. **2.** Trace two punching designs as given, plus a separate repeat of the V-unit 2″ below on each. Tape tracings to left and right fronts about 3½″ (9 cm) below shoulder seams and about ⅝″ (1.5 cm) from front edges. Punch holes, using medium size for top diamond, medium size for V-shapes and largest hole for others. Remove tracings. **3.** Using medium-size hole, punch holes ⅜″ (1 cm) apart just inside topstitching on front, neck and bottom edges of jacket front only. Punch holes across pocket tops and lower edge of sleeves in same way. **4.** For lacing, cut fabric in long strips about 3/16″ (4 to 5 mm) wide; about 15 yds. (13.8 m) will be needed. Cut ends of strips diagonally. **5.** Using tapestry needle, lace strips through holes of V-shapes as shown in diagram, weaving ends through lacing on wrong side. **6.** Lace strips along edges of jacket, pockets and sleeves. Begin and end strips by weaving ends under lacing on wrong side. When complete, secure all ends with a drop of fabric glue. **7.** Ties: Cut four 30″ (76 cm) strips of fabric. Draw one strip through a hole on front edge opposite lacing of middle V. Pull ends even and tie a knot close to jacket. Attach another strip opposite bottom V. Repeat this procedure for other side.

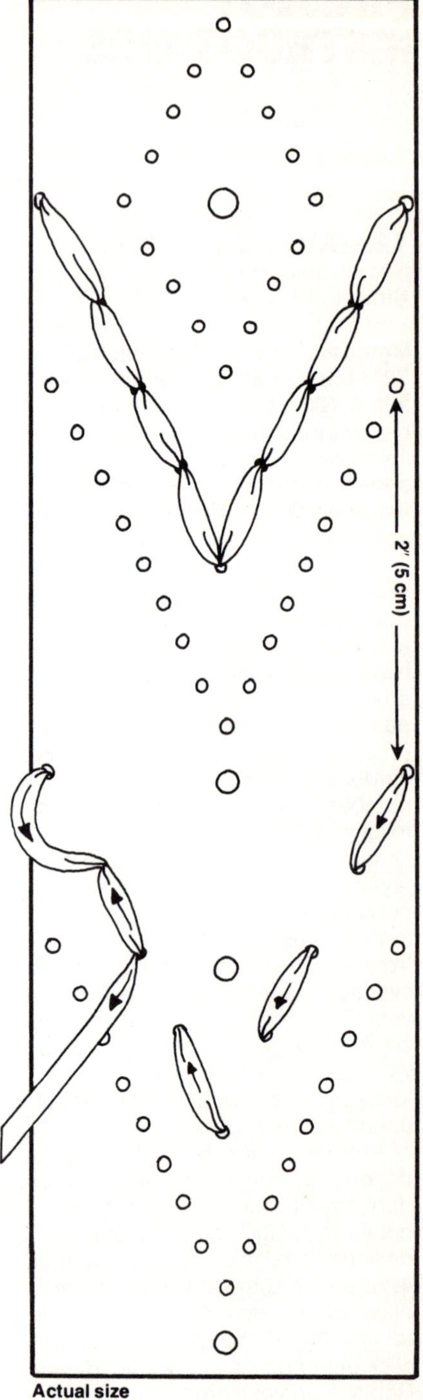

Actual size

IDEA FILE

Special fabrics make creative sewing a breeze. Dramatic prints need only a careful layout; non-ravel fabrics only the right finishing; mixtures only to be combined with flair. How the fabric is used is what counts! Here, more ideas.

Flatter yourself. Use a dramatic border print across the yoke of a tunic...simple to do and very effective.♥

Too lovely to keep under cover, sheeting by-the-yard is stretched on a frame to make a bold and striking wall hanging.♥

Pants go Western style—with yoke and fringe cut in one piece. Use mock leather or suede, and there's no raveling, no finishing needed.♥

Place the wrapped edge of a simple pattern (just two pieces here) on a smashing border print to achieve a flattering vertical line perfect for any figure.♥

The decorative edge of eyelet creates the prettiest border for a frothy cover-up—eliminates facings too.♥♥

Practice the art of print mixing on a carryall. Pick a small floral for some parts and larger ones for the rest.♥

SAY IT WITH STITCHERY

SEWING PLUS

Here's a small sampling of what's possible when sewing teams up with creative stitchery, from simple hand stitches to the easiest machine embroidery.

17 Automatic machine embroidery stitches add colorful new stripes to Dad's western-yoked shirt.♥

18 Friendly pairs of simply-stitched cats sit along a grassy border on this little girl's dress.♥♥

19 Delicate cross-stitch embroidery decorates Mother's apron bib. It's quick to do by hand on even-weave Aida cloth.♥♥♥

20 Even the table wears its own finery—a cloth with modern-day cutwork, done by machine zigzagging and snipping away.♥♥

For instructions see pages 52-54

8133

8092

8114

SAY IT WITH STITCHERY

A few simple stitches can create lots of design variety and textural interest. Here, bold designs and bright colors on accessories made for you and your home.

21 Gobelin-stitched pocket picks up the Aztec-inspired color and design theme of the tabard fabric. ♥♥♥

22 Yarn overcasting plus X's are a brand-new—and super-fast—way to add color and texture to a stylish peasant belt. ♥

23 Free motion machine embroidery gives this roomy tote so much personality, you'll want to take it along everywhere. ♥♥

24 Abstract punchwork design does nice things for this plush decorator pillow. Why not make a pretty pair! ♥♥

See pages 55-56 for directions

SAY IT WITH STITCHERY

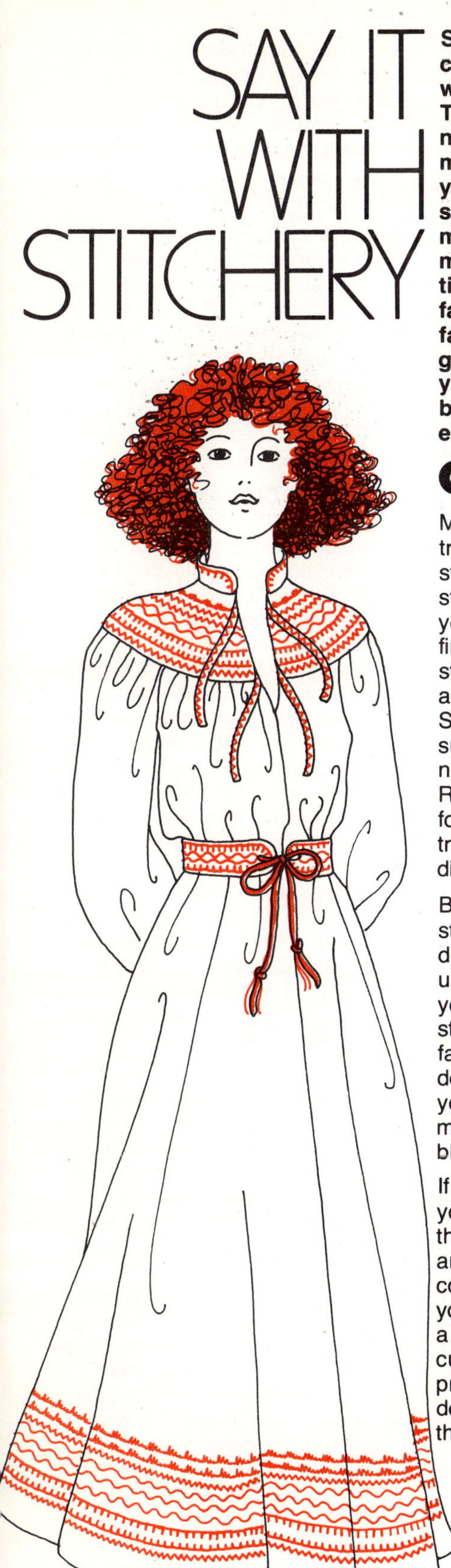

Stitchery is a broad term that covers any decorative work done with needle and thread. Techniques include embroidery, needlepoint, punchwork and many more. Because we know your time is valuable, we've selected quick, easy stitchery methods—those that will produce maximum results in very little time. Even if you use only the fastest, simplest techniques, the fashions, home furnishings and gifts you sew will sparkle with your creative personality because stitchery makes them extra-special!

GENERAL HINTS

Many Simplicity patterns come with transfers for embroidery or other stitchery. Use them as is or as a starting point for a design venture of your own. If you use a pattern, you'll find specific instructions for the stitches and kind of thread to use, and suggestions for suitable fabrics. Sometimes the technique itself will suggest a design, such as needlepoint done in geometrics. Read Design Decisions, pages 5-12, for more design ideas and ways to transfer your own designs to different fabric types.

Be sure that all materials for your stitchery project are compatible in design and care requirements. Don't use wool yarn to embroider a dress you'll wash or delicate thread and stitches on coarse, loosely-woven fabric. Do make sure that the decorative details will complement your garment—such as shimmery metallic threads embroidering a long black party dress.

If possible, do the stitchery before you assemble the project. This way, the work is easier to manage and any raw edges or loose ends can be concealed in seams. If the section you're working on is too small to fit in a hoop, do the stitchery before cutting it out. It's also a good idea to preshrink any fabric you plan to decorate with stitchery, especially if the finished item will be laundered.

MACHINE EMBROIDERY

Fancy stitches marching across fabric? Well, maybe. But machine embroidery is a lot more than that! Though they're a good starting point, automatic decorative stitches aren't necessary for really spectacular results. With a little help from you, ordinary straight or zigzag stitches can transform a garment from simple to super in practically no time (A). Special designs for machine embroidery are available, but you can convert any design into a machine-embroidered masterpiece. To start, use a simple design with gradual curves; transfer it to your fabric as directed on page 7.

There are two types of machine embroidery. One is like regular sewing with a variety of stitches and threads. The other is free motion embroidery done without a presser foot or the machine feed. Your hands move the stretched fabric as the machine stitches. With either kind of embroidery, you can use straight, zigzag or automatic stitches.

GETTING STARTED

Before you start any machine embroidery project, familiarize yourself with the technique. Use this practice period to find the best combination of thread, needle, fabric, tension and pressure; write them down so you can refer to them each time you do a project. There are no hard-and-fast rules about these variables because they depend on your project and especially on your particular sewing machine. The following suggestions will be helpful.

- Choose a firmly-woven, light to medium-weight fabric or stable knit.
- After transferring the design to the fabric, back it with a lightweight woven fabric or fuse lightweight iron-on interfacing to the wrong side to keep fabric from stretching as you work. You can also stabilize a lightweight fabric for easier handling by spray-starching and pressing, or by stitching with tissue underneath it.
- Consult your machine instruction manual for information on using special stitches, adjusting tension and disengaging the feed for free motion embroidery.

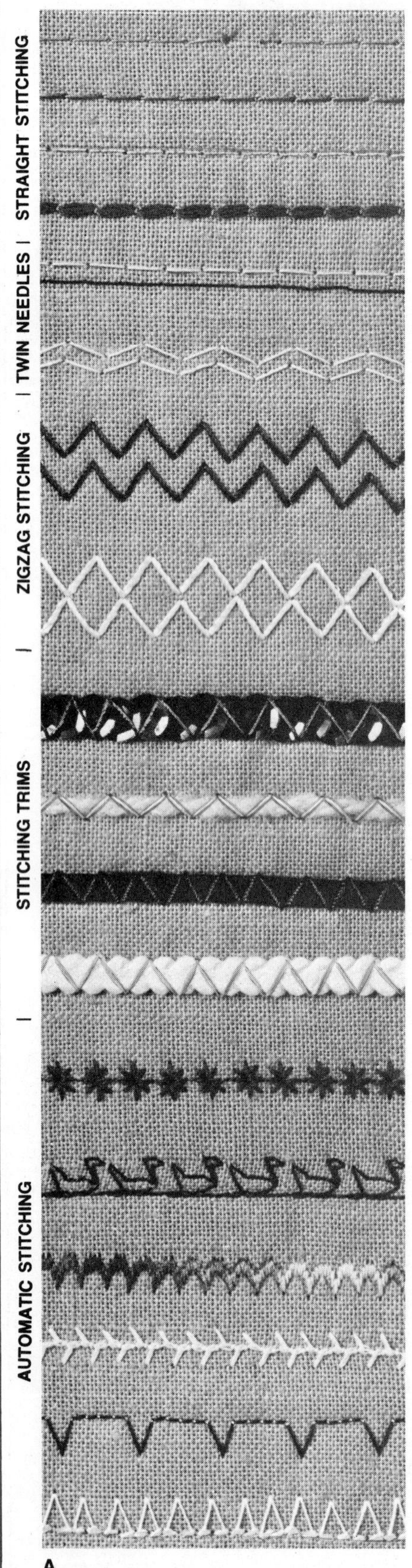

A

- Be sure your machine is in top condition—clean and well-oiled.
- Use a sharp, new needle large enough for your thread.
- Be sure the thread shows up on the fabric.
- Test all your variables until you get the right combination of thread, stitch length and tension.
- Try to attend a demonstration of free motion embroidery in a local sewing machine store or fabric shop, or else plan to spend some time experimenting until you get the feel of the technique and the effects you can achieve with it.

REGULAR MACHINE EMBROIDERY

Regular machine stitching can create many different decorative effects—striped or checkered designs, areas filled in by stitching over yarn or cord, outlines made by stitching around simple designs.

Straight and Zigzag Stitches: The many creative effects you can obtain with basic straight or zigzag stitching are explained below.

Straight stitches take on many personalities with different threads. You can use mercerized cotton or polyester thread, polyester buttonhole twist, pearl cotton, metallic or ombré thread, or embroidery floss (A). Since pearl cotton and embroidery floss are too heavy to go through the needle, you must wind them onto the bobbin; then, stitch on the wrong side of the fabric so the heavier thread will be on the right side. Most straight stitching is used to outline, but multiple rows, especially those done with heavier threads, can make a pretty border design (A).

Zigzag stitches can be worked with any of the threads just mentioned. Stitch them with the points matching, or make the points meet to form diamonds (A). For outlines, space the stitches closely (satin stitch) (D); for filling, space them more openly. Zigzag over sequins on a string, narrow braid, yarn or satin cord (A). Set the stitch width so it just catches the outer edge of the sequins; stitch in the direction sequins overlap. Stitch over other trims in the same way. Use these for outlining or for filling an area. You can also combine zigzag and satin stitching with appliqué and patchwork.

Twin Needles: These will more than double your creativity. With any stitch—straight, zigzag or fancy—you can use the same or different colors of threads. Twin needle zigzag stitches are especially effective for filling in an area (A).

Automatic Stitches: Many sewing machines can do decorative stitch designs such as stars, animals and scallops (A, D). In plain or ombré thread, these stitches can outline or fill an area (A). And don't overlook the decorative potential of stretch, blind-hem or other more functional stitches. Use them as you would fancy stitches (A).

FREE MOTION MACHINE EMBROIDERY

This technique takes a bit of practice, but the results are well worth the time it takes to learn. Using free motion instead of hand embroidery, you can add your own special flair to clothes (B). To begin, loosen the upper tension. Set the machine for straight stitch or zigzag, with stitch length at 0. Remove the presser foot and disengage or cover the feed. Use a 6 to 8″ (15 to 20.5 cm) embroidery hoop as follows: Place the larger ring on the bed of the machine, position fabric over it and snap in the smaller ring. On some machines, you may have to remove the needle to do this. Keep fabric *very taut*! And remember to lower the presser foot bar *to engage the upper tension* before you start to stitch.

Keep fingers close to the needle to hold the fabric down; start stitching, moving hoop slowly, and follow the design outline (C). Overlap the first few stitches to lock threads. Don't move suddenly or the thread—or needle—may break. Always keep the design in line with the feed. For zigzag stitching, move fabric forward slightly, blending stitches as you go, then from side to side as needed to follow design lines. When lines cross, make the first line of stitching less dense and the second more prominent. For parallel zigzag stitches, keep the work straight; for thick and thin lines, change the angle of approach as you feed the fabric (E). Don't limit yourself to filling in; as you become more adept, try swirls, flowers and initials (F).

B
C
D
E
F

MACHINE CUTWORK

With your sewing machine doing most of the work, you can create an airy, open design on a garment (A), or on decorator accessories such as pillowcases or tablecloths. You can use light to medium-weight woven fabric or a stable double knit, and

A

matching or contrasting thread. If desired, back the fabric with a fusible interfacing for stability and to prevent puckering on lightweight fabrics.

Transfer the design you've selected to your fabric as directed in Design Decisions, page 7.

If you've backed your fabric, first staystitch over the traced lines and, with sharp, pointed scissors, cut the fabric inside the staystitching close to the stitching (B). Then satin-stitch (close zigzag) over the staystitching along the cut edge (C). Trim away any loose threads.

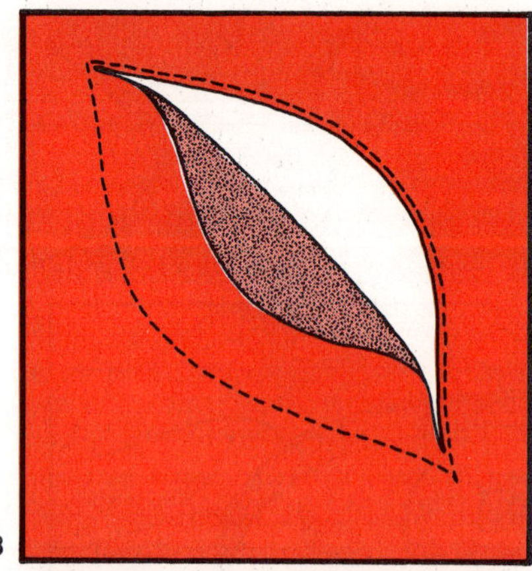
B

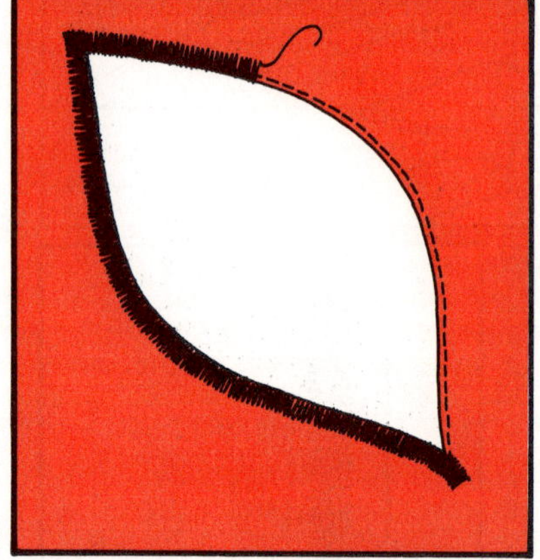
C

On fabric that has not been backed, first satin-stitch along the traced lines and then cut the fabric away, carefully trimming raveled ends.

To cover a larger area more quickly, as on a tablecloth, combine machine embroidery with cutwork for a very effective design. See our pretty basketweave cutwork tablecloth photographed on page 38. Omit any interfacing where it may show through to the right side. Do all decorative stitching as described above; then cut away only the desired design areas.

TRAPUNTO

Trapunto is a unique form of quilting where only certain areas of a design are stuffed or padded. It's an easy and effective way to add dimension or focus on a fashion detail. The design areas are outlined with stitching first and stuffed later; they may be narrow channels, geometric designs or abstract shapes (D).

D

CHANNEL TRAPUNTO

This type of stitchery is often used at hems and edges of garments to emphasize design lines, and must be done as the hem or edge is being finished. Channels outlining areas not located at edges should be stuffed before the garment is assembled. In addition to the fashion fabric, you'll need a lightweight backing fabric and bulky yarn for filling the stitched lines.

With a chalk pencil, mark stitching lines on the right side of the fabric ¼ to ⅜″ (6 mm to 1 cm) apart. Cut backing as wide as all channels plus any seam allowances on the garment area and ½″ (1.3 cm) extra on either side of channels. Pin backing to wrong side; then stitch along marked lines with matching thread. If you're making channels at a hemline (of a jacket or sleeve, for example) you can use the hem allowance as the backing. Just be sure to allow enough depth in the hem allowance when cutting out to accommodate all the channels.

To stuff, thread a yarn needle with bulky yarn, slit backing at channel if

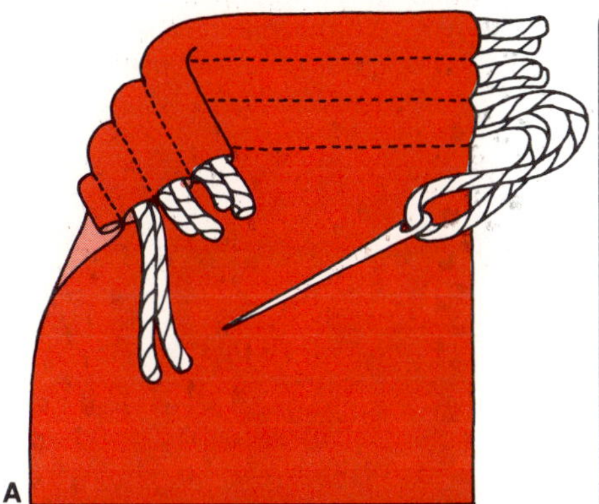

A

necessary, and draw yarn through channels (A). At seam allowances, stitch across each end of channels to secure the yarn, then trim ends. Close slits with a fused patch or slipstitching. To go around sharp curves or corners, bring needle out of the channel, leave a small loop of yarn outside corner, slit backing, then push needle back into the channel on the next side.

FREE-FORM TRAPUNTO

For a garment or a pillow, you might want to stuff a single motif or a series of motifs like floral or animal shapes. Mark, back and stitch just as for channel trapunto. To stuff, slit the backing and insert polyester fiberfill until the shapes stand out nicely on the right side (B). Slipstitch or fuse a patch on slits to close.

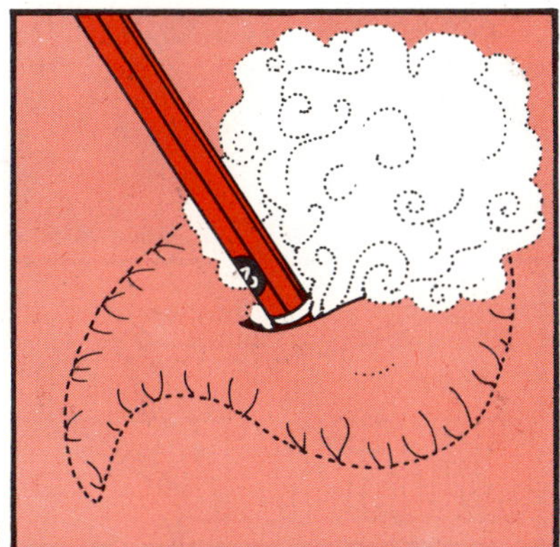

B

HAND EMBROIDERY

Everyone admires the rich look of hand embroidery, from bold yarn painting to delicate cross-stitch. Although there are dozens of stitches, we've chosen ones that are simple to do and cover a lot of territory quickly. They can outline,

C

highlight, edge or fill in an area (C). Read General Hints, page 41.

EQUIPMENT

Yarns and Needles: There are many threads and yarns which produce various effects depending on the stitches used. Six-strand embroidery floss can be separated into strands for finer or heavier embroidery. Pearl cotton has a slight sheen and comes in various weights. Matte-finish cotton is a bit heavier and has no sheen. For crewel embroidery, the favorite is Persian-type yarn, three strands of wool lightly twisted together that can be separated. Novelty threads for special effects include silk, rayon, linen, metallics and straw-like yarns.

For embroidery, use a crewel or embroidery needle in the right size for your yarn or thread; it should pierce the fabric easily without leaving a hole. Crewel needles have sharp points and long eyes for easy threading. They come in different sizes, designated by numbers. The higher the number, the finer the needle. Keep an assortment so you'll always have the right needle.

Other Supplies: Use an embroidery hoop to keep fabric taut; otherwise the stitches will pucker the fabric. Wear a thimble for protection against needle stabs, and use small, sharp, pointed scissors for snipping threads.

STITCHES

There are many fast and easy hand embroidery stitches. The most versatile are explained here.

Cross-Stitch: Work in rows from left to right. Keeping needle straight, insert needle at equal intervals, forming slanted half-crosses. Then, working from right to left, complete crosses by inserting needle in same way as before (D).

Cross-stitch may be used for borders and solid filling. You can work it on mesh-like fabrics such as Aida cloth, where the holes in the fabric act as a guide for placing the stitches, indicated on a graph like the one shown on page 53. It may also be worked from a cross-stitch transfer pattern design.

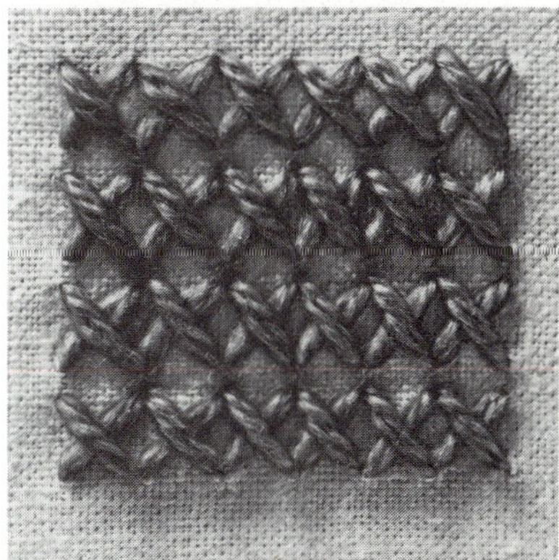

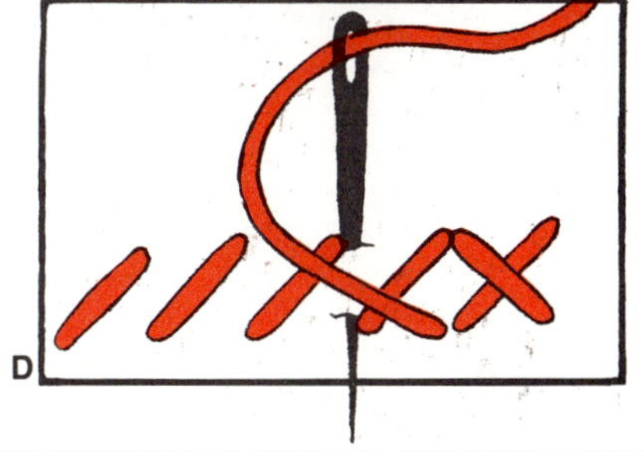

D

Chain Stitch: This stitch makes a decorative outline, stems for flowers or, worked in close rows, a solid filling. Work from the top of line. Make a loop with thread and hold it in place with left thumb. Insert needle right where thread first came up. Holding loop down with thumb, bring needle out a short distance ahead on line, over loop (A).

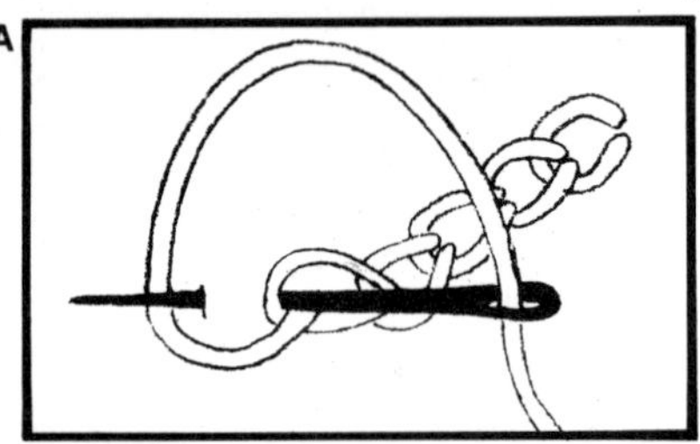

Backstitch: This stitch can make a sharp outline or a solid filling. Work from right to left. Bring thread up on line and insert needle a little to the right. Now bring needle up again an equal distance ahead. Insert again at beginning of last stitch (B).

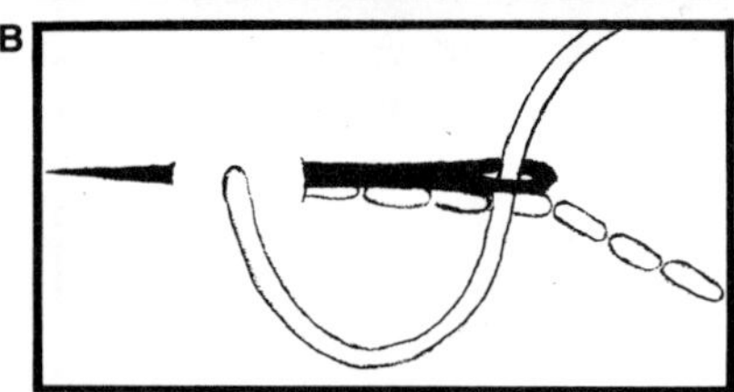

Running Stitch: This stitch is used for lines and outlines. Work from right to left. Be sure that each stitch is identical in size and the spaces between are the same. Do not make a series of stitches at one time (C).

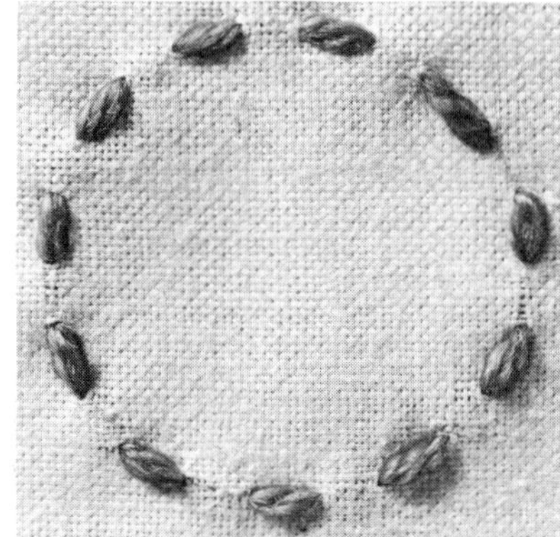

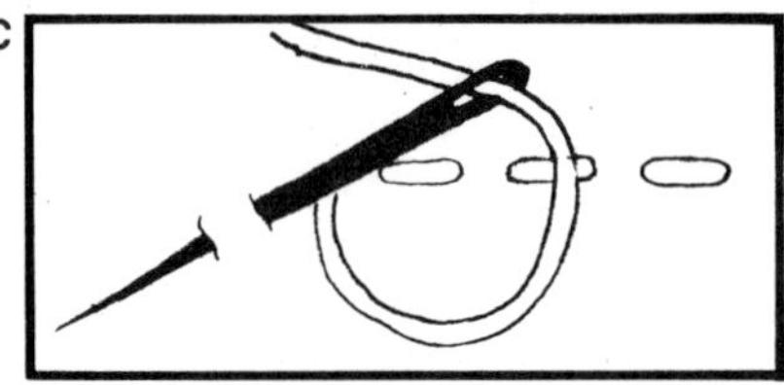

Straight Stitch: This stitch may be used singly to form a detail such as a stem or a blade of grass; or a group of straight stitches may be worked close together, or somewhat spaced, to fill in an area. This stitch can also make flowers. Work in any direction. Bring needle up through fabric and insert it straight down to make a stitch of the desired length (D).

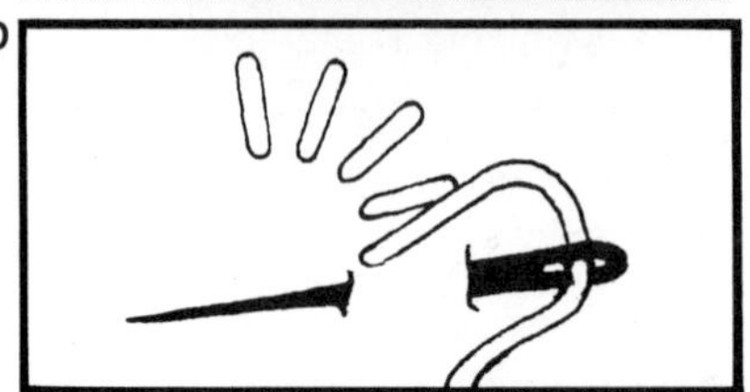

Blanket Stitch: This is a multi-purpose stitch. It can form outlines, be used for filling, cover an edge of fabric or form a flower when worked in a circle. Work from left to right. Bring needle up and hold loop of thread down with left thumb. Keeping needle straight, insert it at equal intervals, and bring it out over loop of thread, forming a vertical stitch as in diagram (E). Stitches can be spaced anywhere from 1/8 to 3/8" (3 mm to 10 mm) apart, depending on the thickness of thread used (E).

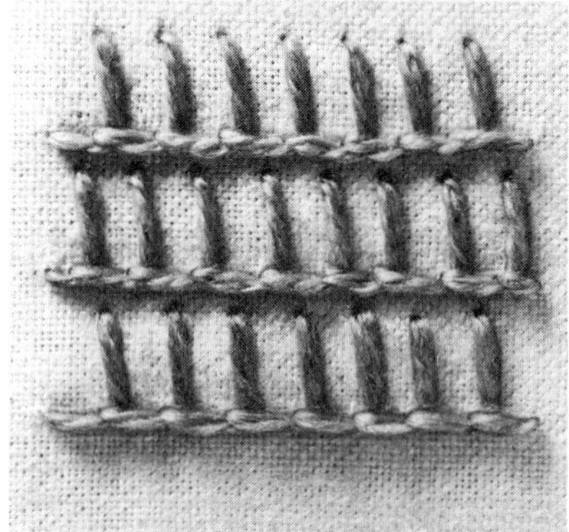

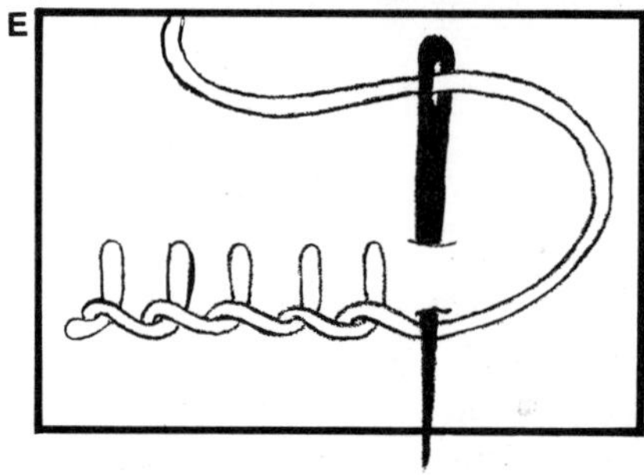

Overcast Stitch: This stitch is used to finish and decorate edges. Work from left to right, taking stitches over the edge that are straight up and down and right next to each other or space stitches widely (F).

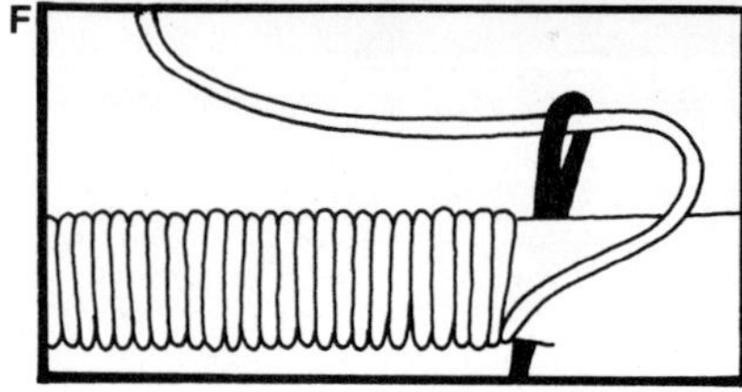

Feather Stitch: This stitch is used for border designs, lines and, very occasionally, for filling. Start a little to left of guideline. Holding thread with left thumb, work a small slanting stitch at the right and a bit below where thread emerged. Needle points to the left. Pull needle through over thread loop. Make thread loop on left of guideline and work a stitch as before but with needle pointing to right. Pull needle through over loop formed by thread (A).

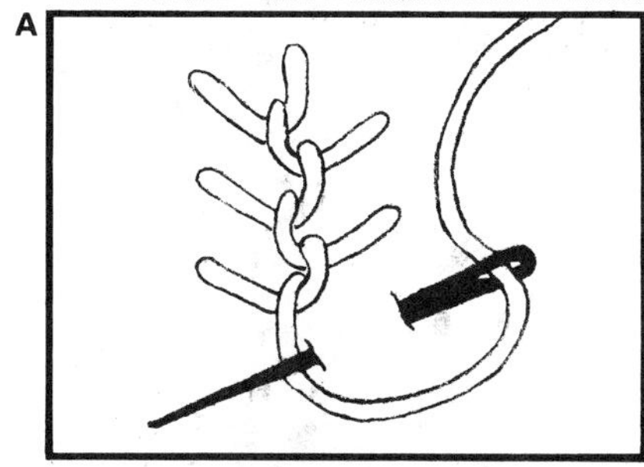

A

Herringbone Stitch: This stitch is used for borders. Work from left to right. Bring thread out at left end of lower guideline. Make a small stitch from right to left on upper guideline. Make a similar stitch from right to left on lower guideline. Repeat. Keep stitches very even (B).

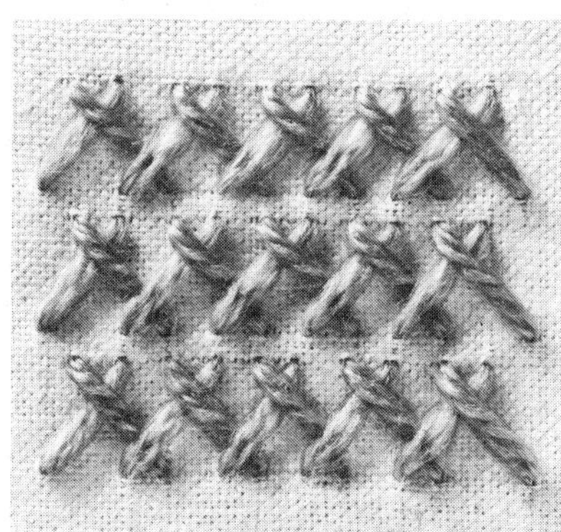

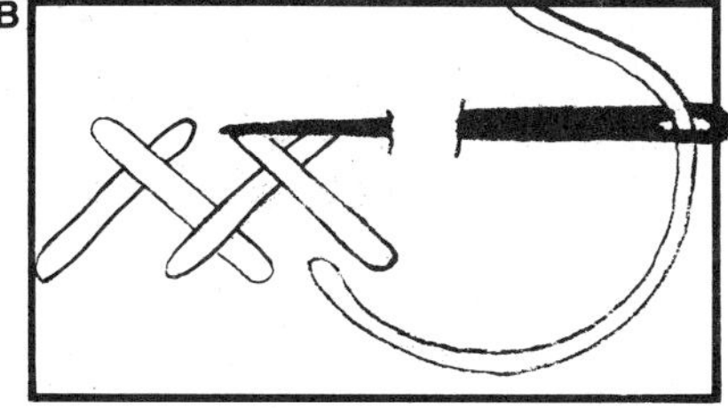

B

Lazy-Daisy Stitch: This is also known as Detached Chain Stitch. Worked in a circle, Lazy-Daisy Stitches make charming flowers. Worked separately, they may be used to form individual petals or a light filling stitch. Try embroidering a row of Lazy-Daisy Stitch flowers along a hemline of a skirt or dress for a pretty floral border.

Bring the thread up and hold it in a loop with the left thumb. Insert needle back where the thread emerged. Then bring the needle out the length of the stitch desired and pull it through over the loop. Make a small straight stitch to anchor the loop at its crown (C).

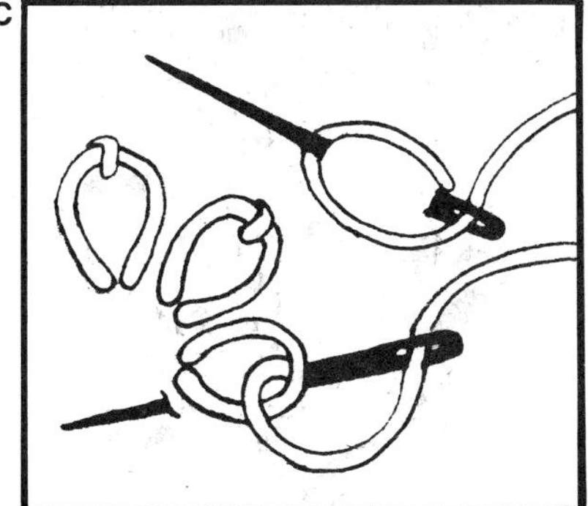

C

Stem Stitch: This is a basic stitch used for lines, outlines and the stems of flowers. Work from left to right. Start at left end of guideline and make a small stitch, slanting it slightly across guideline. Be sure to keep thread below the needle throughout. If the thread is held above the needle throughout, the stitch is called Outline Stitch. Note the interesting effect you get when you make a stitch with the thread above the needle and the next stitch with the thread below the needle (D).

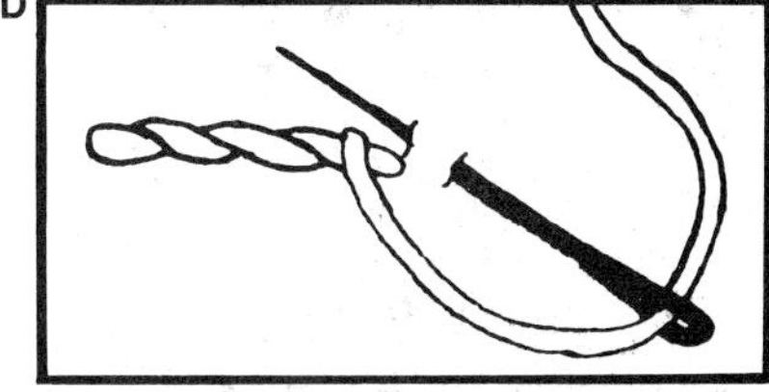

D

FINISHING

After you've completed the embroidery, but before you end it off, why not sign your name or your initials in stitches? Then finish. Place the piece face down on the ironing board, which you've padded with a terrycloth towel. Then press it lightly with a steam iron or dry iron and damp press cloth. Don't let the iron rest heavily on the embroidered areas or you'll flatten the stitches. You can press the margins of the piece where there is no embroidery in the usual way.

Now you are ready to use your stitchery to decorate a garment, pillow, wall hanging, or other home furnishing accessory.

PUNCH-NEEDLE WORK

A

We usually think of punch-needle work as a method of hooking rugs, which it is. But it's also a way to add textural interest to pillows, wall hangings, or seat covers. See our color-splashed pillow on page 40. Use it on clothing and fashion accessories as well (A). Picture a punchwork design on the back of a denim jacket, forming pockets on a vest or jumper, or playing up the front of an unusual-looking tabard.

MATERIALS

To do punchwork, you'll need a coarsely-woven backing fabric such as burlap, monk's cloth or unbleached cotton, a punch needle, a large embroidery hoop or canvas stretcher to keep the fabric taut and medium-weight yarn.

PUNCHING

When punching, work on the wrong side of the fabric, forming loops on the right side. Some punch needles make loops of one size only. Others allow you to adjust the height of the loops for a sculptured effect. Since you work on the wrong side, reverse the design (unless it's reversible) and transfer it to the *wrong side.*

Cut your fabric 2″ (5 cm) larger all around than the finished size and stretch it, wrong side up, in a hoop or stretcher. Thread punch needle with yarn and begin by outlining an area in the center of the work.

Punch the needle through to the right side as far as it will go, then slowly withdraw it to the wrong side, without raising it from the surface of the fabric. Move the needle a few strands away and punch again. You may find it helpful to hold yarn loops on the right side as you work. Continue to work until outline is complete. Then fill in the area, working in rows or at random (B).

Keep stitches close enough together so that no fabric shows between the loops on the right side, but loose enough to avoid making the work very stiff (C). As you develop a feel for the technique, the work will begin to go quickly and you'll find that large areas can be filled in easily.

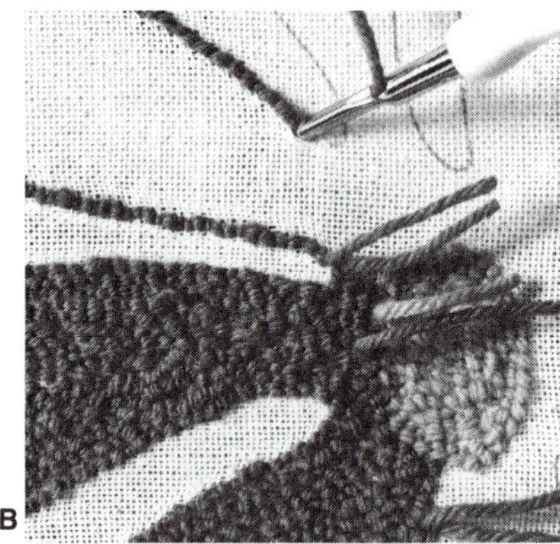

B

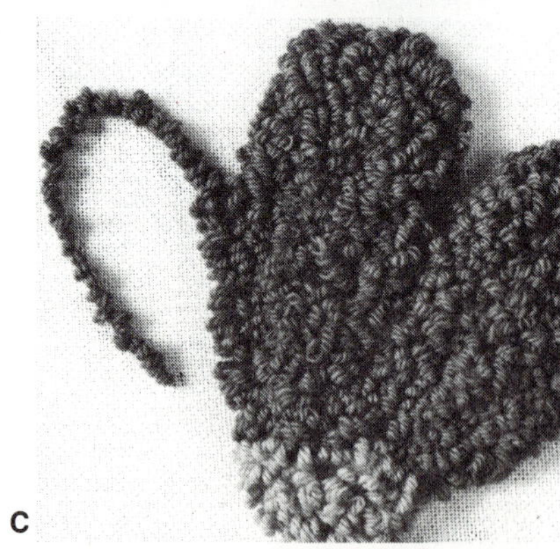

C

FINISHING

For a rug or wall hanging, coat the back with latex rug adhesive before removing it from the frame to keep stitches anchored. Let coating dry. Hem, or apply rug binding. For a garment, cut a lining the same size as punched fabric; pin to the wrong side. Mark seam line, then staystitch layers together; trim away excess fabric ⅝″ (1.5 cm) from seam line. Assemble project with a zipper foot.

NEEDLEPOINT

Needlepoint is a kind of embroidery worked on open mesh canvas. It's a pleasurable technique that can produce an almost unbelievable variety of designs. Since many of these stitches are such speedy techniques, they're ideal for making vests, pockets, bags, yokes or pillows in a hurry (D, E).

Needlepoint is classified according to the gauge of the canvas—the number of meshes per inch. Petitpoint, very fine needlepoint, is done on canvas with 16 or more meshes per inch; grospoint on 8 to 15 meshes; and quickpoint, a very fast method, is worked on 3½ to 7

D

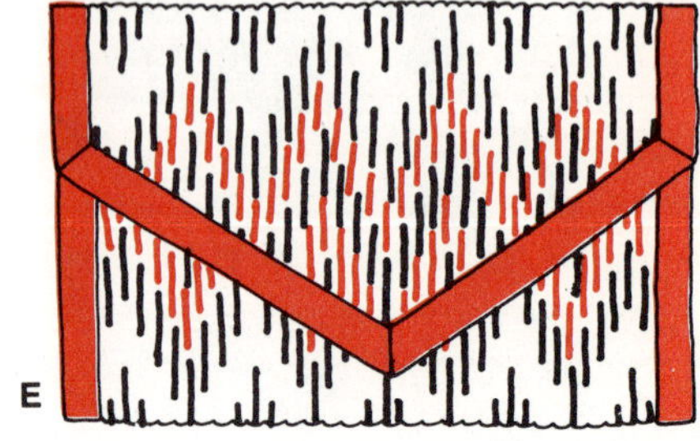

E

meshes per inch (2.5 cm) (A, B). Using bulky yarn and Half Cross or Continental Stitch, page 50, you can create an eyecatching quickpoint design in a very short time.

For other fast needlepoint stitches, see Bargello and Gobelin Stitch, pages 50-51.

MATERIALS

Canvas: There are two main types—single-mesh or mono (C), and double-mesh or Penelope (D) canvas. Since the latter is more durable, it's better for a project that might be subjected to wear and tear.

A new type of canvas, made of nylon, differs from regular canvas. A single-mesh type, it's flexible and can be worked in a hoop. Unlike regular canvas, which must be dry-cleaned, it is washable. If you work with washable yarn on nylon canvas, it can be laundered.

Yarns and Thread: Yarns for doing needlepoint include tapestry wool, Persian-type yarn (also used for doing crewel embroidery) and cotton floss. Both come in a wide range of colors. For special effects, there's silk thread, shiny satin cord or velvety velour thread. For doing quickpoint, wool or acrylic rug yarn is best, since it's a bulky yarn made especially for this purpose. Knitting yarns are not recommended for needlepoint because they are not strong enough to withstand repeated pulling through canvas, and they may become fuzzy. Whatever yarn you choose (E), be sure that it is compatible with the canvas size.

The object of needlepoint is to cover the canvas completely without crowding the stitches.

A GROSPOINT AND PETITPOINT

B QUICKPOINT ON PENELOPE CANVAS

C MONO CANVAS

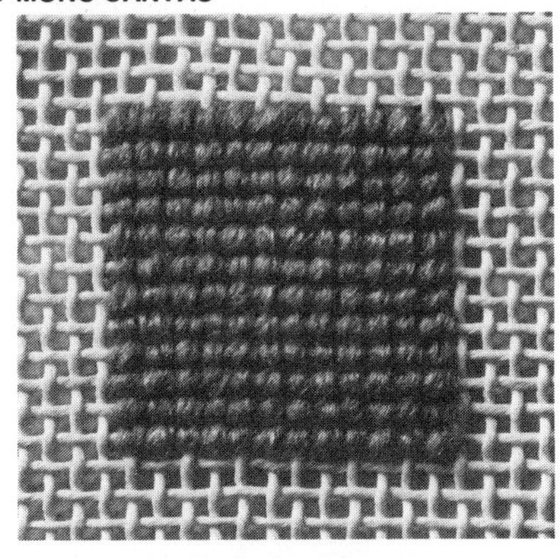

D PENELOPE CANVAS

Amount of Yarn: When using a ready-made design, you are usually given the yarn requirements. For your own design, you can estimate how much you'll need by making a 1" square (2.5 cm) sample in the stitch you plan to use. Note the length of yarn in the needle as you start and what's left when you finish; the difference is the amount used for your sample. Multiply by the finished size to determine total yarn needed (estimate the individual color breakdown). Buy enough yarn at once so you won't have a problem matching color or dye lots later on.

Other Equipment: You'll need an assortment of tapestry needles, which have blunt ends and come in different sizes appropriate for the various thicknesses of yarns.

A canvas stretcher for mounting the canvas while working the needlepoint is optional, but does minimize distortion of the canvas. Without the frame, of course, the canvas is portable, so you can take it wherever you go. You should also have small, sharp, pointed scissors for cutting yarn.

Designs: You can buy needlepoint canvas with a design already stamped. Sometimes the design is tinted to indicate colors to be used. Or you can use a design drawn on a graph-paper chart; each square represents one stitch. If you're using your own design, transfer it to the canvas according to the directions given in Design Decisions, page 7.

E

GETTING STARTED

Cut your canvas 2" (5 cm) larger all around to allow for blocking, seams or turn-under. Bind the edges with masking tape or seam binding to keep them from raveling.

If you plan to quickpoint garment sections (the fronts of a vest, for example), cut a square or rectangle large enough to accommodate the actual pattern pieces. Observing grainlines, trace cutting line and seam line onto the canvas. Then

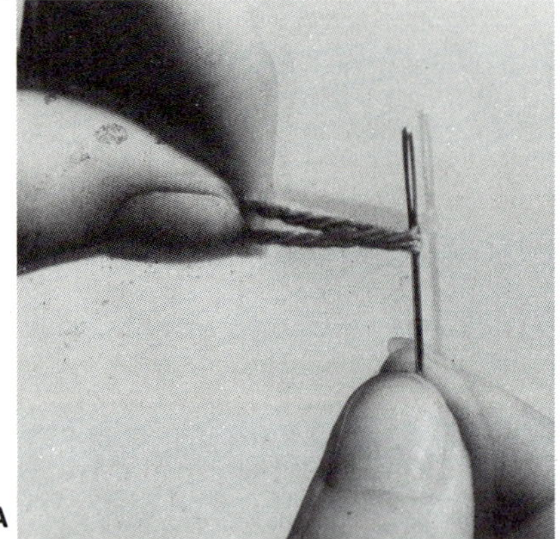

A

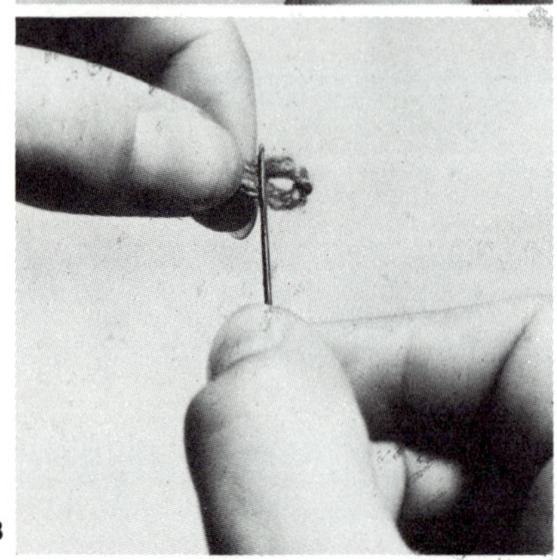

B

work the quickpoint over the entire area inside the seam line. Then finish; see instructions on page 51.

Work with yarn no more than 20″ (51 cm) long. To thread needle, fold yarn over needle (A). Holding fold tightly against needle with thumb and forefinger, pull fold off needle. Still holding tightly, push fold through eye and pull thread through (B).

When working needlepoint stitches, don't pull them too tight or they will not cover the canvas. If the yarn knots or twists, drop threaded needle, allowing the yarn to relax.

Work stitches up and down through the canvas, one stitch at a time. To begin a new strand, weave about 1″ (2.5 cm) through the back of a previous row, or hold it against the back of the row you are working and cover it as you work. Clip loose ends to prevent tangles.

STITCHES

The easiest stitches for quickpoint are the Half Cross and the Continental Stitch. They look the same on the right side (C), but do not look alike on the back because they're done differently.

C

Half Cross Stitch: This stitch uses the least yarn and should not be used on mono canvas (D). Since it leaves little yarn on the back, it does not wear well and should be used only on projects that will not receive a great deal of use.

1. Work first row from lower left corner. Bring needle up (a).
2. Insert needle (b) 1 mesh above and to the right of a. Bring up (a) 1 mesh directly below. Finish row.
3. For second row bring needle up (c) 1 mesh above b. Turn work around and put needle in at (d). Complete second row and turn work. Continue to work this way, turning canvas at start of each row.

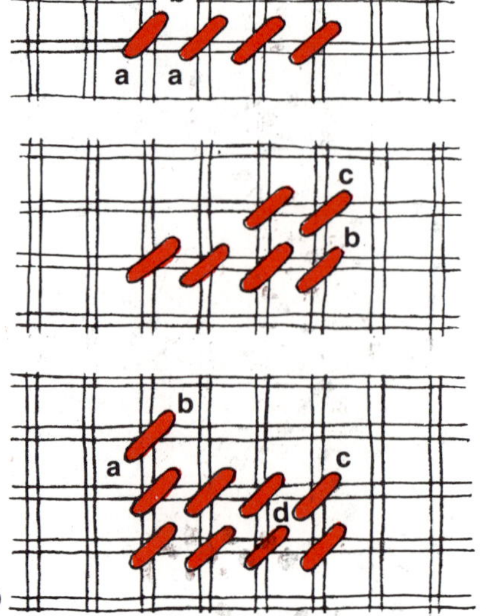

D

Continental Stitch: This is an all-purpose stitch which wears very well (E). Since it distorts the canvas, it requires blocking afterward.

1. Work from right to left. Bring needle up (a).
2. Insert needle (b) 1 mesh above and to the right of a. Bring it up (a) 1 mesh below and 2 meshes to the left of b. Finish row.
3. For second row, bring needle up (c) 1 mesh above b. Turn work around and work same as first row. Continue in the same way, turning canvas at start of each row.

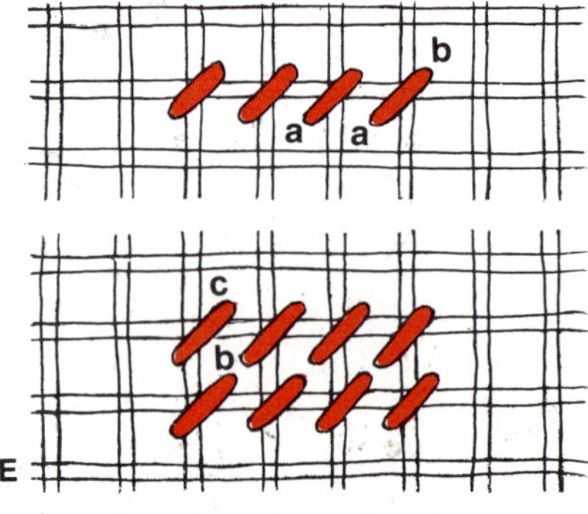

E

Bargello (Florentine Stitch): This is another quick technique; it goes fast because each stitch covers several meshes at a time. With Bargello, you can create striking stair step, block, zigzag (F) or skyscraper shapes. Stitches are worked upright, instead of slanting, over 2, 4 or more meshes, and are often worked in several shades of a single color. The photograph and diagram show one kind of Florentine stitch; you can vary it to make other designs by changing stitch length and color arrangement. Succeeding rows can follow each other or can be worked upside down for diamonds.

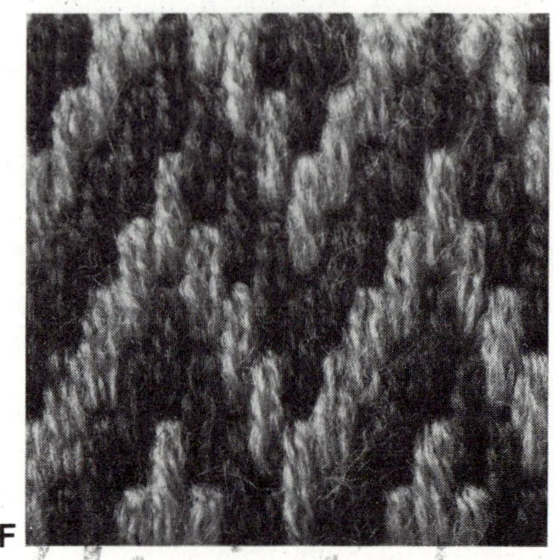

F

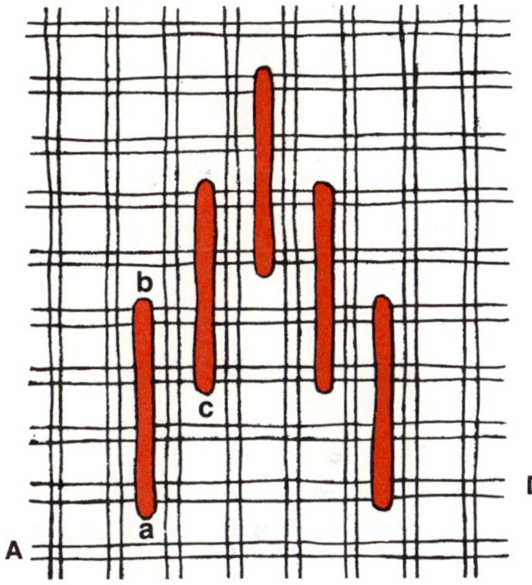

A

Following Bargello diagram (A):
1. Work from left to right. Bring needle up (a).
2. Insert needle (b) 4 meshes above a.
3. Bring it up (c) 2 meshes below and to the right of b. Follow diagram to establish first row of design. Work succeeding rows following first row.

Because the possibilities are so numerous, it's a good idea to plan your Bargello designs on graph paper before you work them, or to make some actual samples. The illustrations will give you more ideas for Bargello (B, C, D). Note that the number of meshes the stitch is worked over can vary.

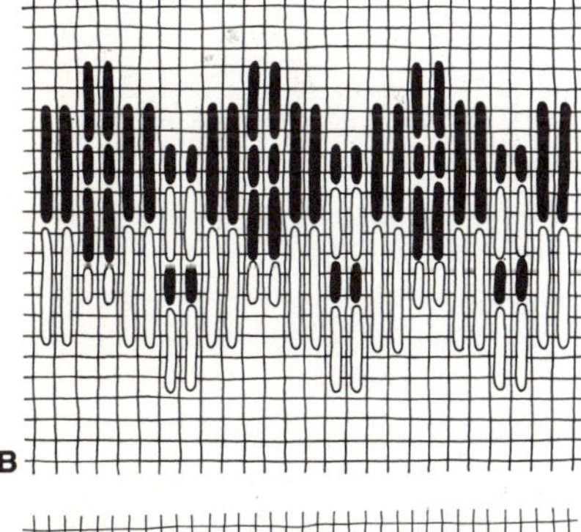

B

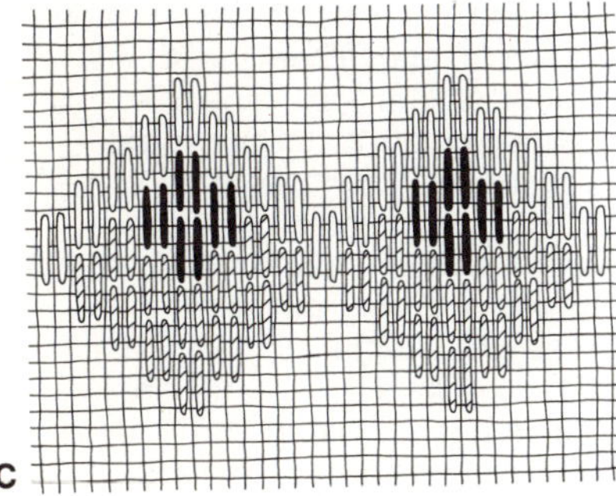

C

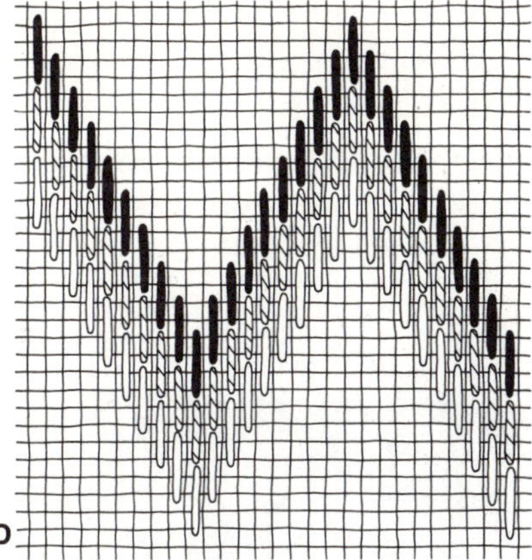

D

Gobelin Stitch: This stitch is easy to do and produces a tapestry-like effect (E). Keep tension fairly loose to insure that the yarn covers the canvas. Gobelin stitch may be worked over 2, 3, 4 or 5 meshes. The diagram (F) shows the stitch done over 3 meshes.

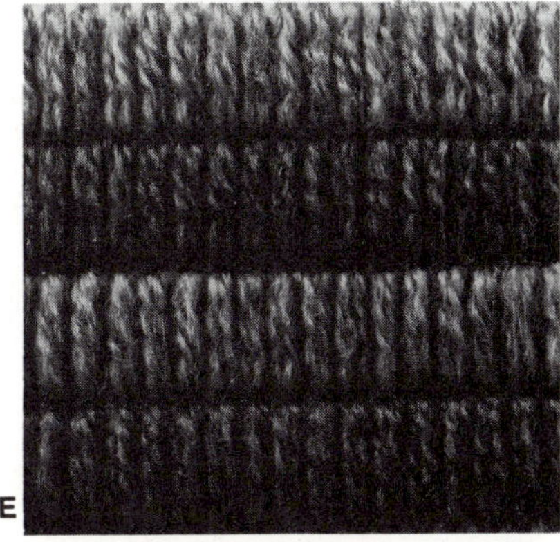

E

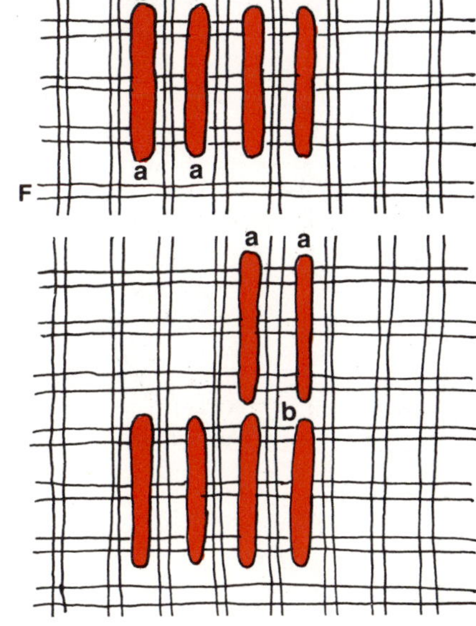

F

1. Work from left to right. Bring needle up (a).
2. Insert (b) 3 meshes directly above a.
3. Bring it out (a) level with and 1 mesh to the right of a. Repeat from Step 2 to finish row. Work next row from right to left.

FINISHING

Whether or not you've worked your needlepoint in a frame, you'll need to block your work when it's completed. Here is a method which works well.

Cover a wooden board, large enough to hold the piece, with brown paper fastened at the corners. Using a ruler, outline the dimensions of the canvas and place needlepoint face down over the paper. Stretching canvas as necessary to fit outline, insert rustproof pushpins 1 to 2" (2.5 to 5 cm) apart (G). Make sure the piece is stretched taut and free of wrinkles. With a clean sponge or cheesecloth, dab water over the needlepointed canvas until it is evenly dampened but not soaked. Let canvas dry *completely* before removing it from the board.

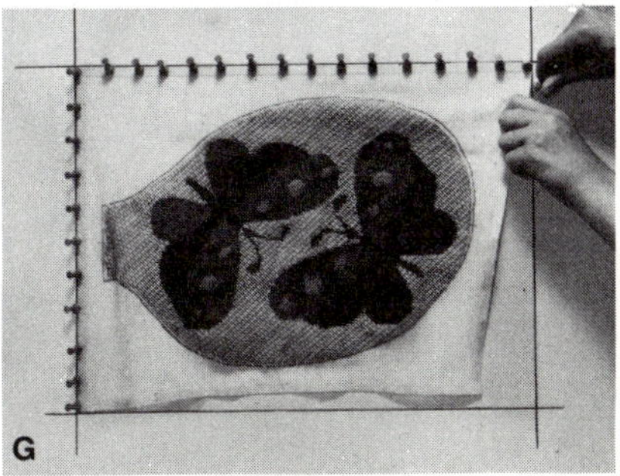

G

To sew a garment section you've needlepointed and blocked, cut out the section on the cutting line previously marked and assemble the garment, using a short stitch and a zipper foot.

For an unlined garment, you can improve wearing comfort by binding the seam allowances of the needlepoint sections. See Binding instructions, page 62. To keep seam allowances flat, you can tack them to the wrong side. If you've made an entire garment of needlepoint, such as a vest, you can finish the edges neatly and decoratively by enclosing them in foldover braid in a coordinating or contrasting color (see page 62).

PROJECT INSTRUCTIONS

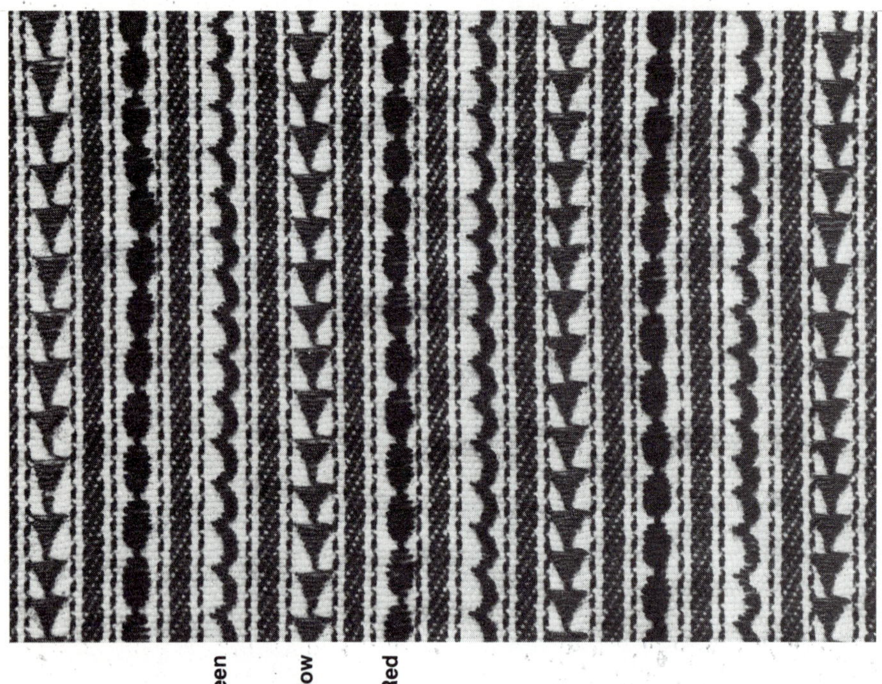

17/WESTERN SHIRT♥

Shown on page 38
Simplicity 8133

Materials: Red, green and yellow thread, striped fabric for shirt.

Directions: 1. Cut shirt out. Before assembling, on front yoke pieces: Do rows of decorative machine stitching on solid white stripes of fabric, following hints for machine embroidery on pages 41 and 42. Use three different decorative stitches and a different thread color for each stitch design; always do the same stitch in the same color.
2. Starting at yoke center front seam line, stitch a green row, then yellow, then red. Repeat this sequence until white stripes on both yoke pieces are covered. Keep sequence for both yoke pieces symmetrical.
3. Complete shirt.

Actual Size

18/CHILD'S EMBROIDERED SUNDRESS ♥♥

Shown on page 39
Simplicity 8092

Materials: Six-strand embroidery floss, 3 skeins blue, 1 skein green; embroidery needle.

Directions: 1. Complete dress. **2.** Trace cat motif and transfer to front and back along border or about 4″ (10 cm) above hemline. **3.** With 2 strands of blue floss in needle, embroider cats as follows: ears, eyes, nose and whiskers with straight stitch, and all other parts with chain stitch (page 46). **4.** With 3 strands of green floss, embroider grass with straight stitch. **5.** With 2 strands of blue floss, work blanket stitch (page 46) along inside and outside edges of shoulder straps.

19/APRON DRESS WITH EMBROIDERY ♥♥♥

Shown on page 39
Simplicity 8114

Key to Colors

Red ●	Yellow
Black /	Lt. Blue
Black +	Med. Blue
Black ●	Dk. Blue

Materials for finished embroidery about 7″ w x 6½″ l (18 x 16.3 cm): ¼ yard (0.25 m) #14 Aida Cloth; six-strand embroidery floss, 2 skeins dark blue, 1 skein each medium blue, light blue and yellow; embroidery needle.

Directions: 1. Complete apron. **2.** Using 3 strands of floss in needle and cross-stitch (page 45), work embroidery following chart. Do not work empty squares on chart. **3.** Press embroidery lightly on wrong side. Turn edges under ⅛″ (3 mm) from outer rows of embroidery and press. Leaving ⅝″ (1.5 cm) margin, trim away excess fabric. **4.** Pin embroidered patch to bib of dress. Baste or fuse in place, then machine-edgestitch to bib.

20/CUTWORK TABLECLOTH ♥♥

Shown on page 38

Materials: Tablecloth and 4 napkins, 4 large spools of thread.

Directions: 1. For lightweight fabric that you can see through, trace designs onto paper with marking pen so they are highly visible. Place design under fabric and trace lightly with pencil, aligning design with fabric grain where possible. For other fabrics, transfer design to fabric by one of the methods given on page 7. Position tablecloth design at *each* corner, 2″ (5 cm) from edges; napkin design at *one* corner, 1¼″ (3.2 cm) from edges. **2.** Wind 2 or 3 bobbins with thread. Following general hints on page 41, satin-stitch over marked lines, working all rows in one direction before starting in another direction. Lock stitches at beginning and end of each row by making 3 stitches with stitch length set on 0. With small, sharp, pointed scissors, carefully cut out all small squares formed by the stitching.

21/TABARD WITH GOBELIN STITCH POCKET ♥♥♥

Shown on page 40
Simplicity 8165

Materials: ¼ yard (0.25 m) # 14 nylon canvas; six-strand embroidery floss, 2 skeins each yellow and blue, 3 green, 5 black, 4 red (or colors to match your fabric); tapestry needle.

Directions: 1. Complete tabard. **2.** Pocket: With 8 strands of floss in needle, use Gobelin stitch (page 51) to work design according to chart. Chart is for ¼ of design. Most rows are worked over 4 to 6 meshes; a few are worked over 5. When piece

Actual Size **Pink area is napkin pattern**

is completed, block as directed on page 51. **3.** Turn canvas to wrong side along edge of embroidery; leaving 1″ (2.5 cm) margin, trim away excess. **4.** Center pocket on front of tabard with lower edge 2¼″ (5.6 cm) above hemline, or where it looks best. Pin or baste in place, then machine-edgestitch side and bottom edges to tabard.

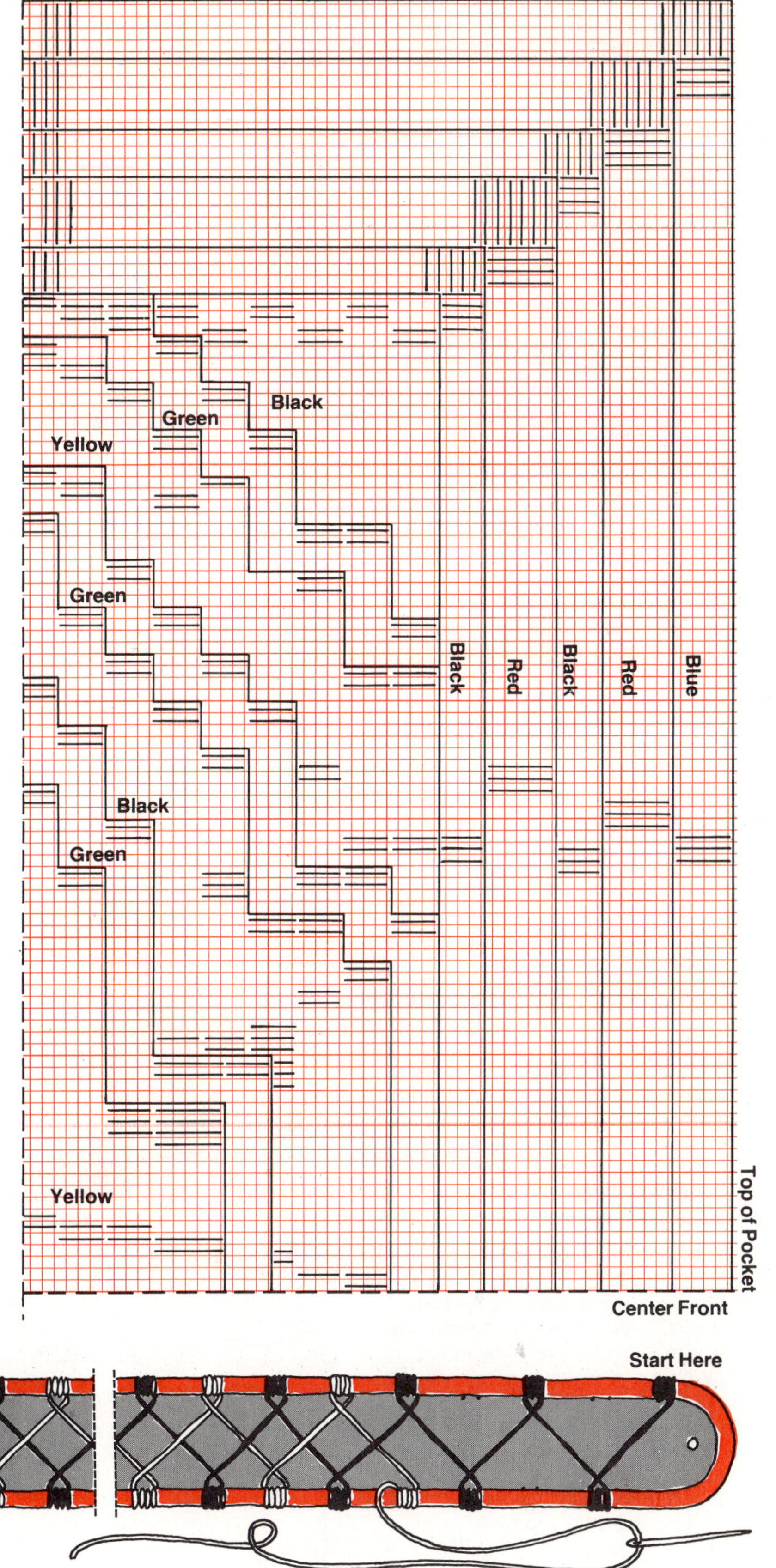

22/CRISS-CROSS TIE BELT♥

Shown on page 40
Simplicity 7919

Materials (for small waist): About 6 yards of yarn in each of 2 contrasting colors; crewel needle.

Directions: 1. Complete belt.
2. Start at center back and mark pairs of pencil dots ½″ (1.3 cm) apart along each edge of belt, working toward ends of belt and spacing pairs 1″ (2.5 cm) apart, until there are 24 pairs on each edge.
3. Thread needle with a strand of yarn and fasten on underside of one end of belt. Starting with first pair of dots, work 6 closely-spaced overcast stitches (page 46) from left dot to right dot over the binding. Bring needle to right side of belt at base of last stitch. **4.** Carry yarn across to next pair of dots diagonally opposite (skipping a pair of dots) and work 6 overcast stitches from left dot to right dot. Carry yarn across to next pair of dots diagonally opposite and work as before (see diagram). Continue in same way to other end of belt. **5.** With second color, turn belt around and work overcasting over remaining pairs of dots in same way. When carrying yarn across belt, weave alternating strands under every other strand of first color.

Start Here

23/MACHINE-EMBROIDERED TOTE ♥♥

Shown on page 40
Simplicity 7004

Materials: Large spools of thread—2 black, 3 green, 4 red; batting.

Directions: 1. Cut out bag. Cut batting from K. Trace and transfer design to bag. On diagram, vertical dotted line marks ½ of design; horizontal lines mark one repeat. Assemble bag up to handles and tabs. Sandwich batting between fabric layers and baste layers as directed on page 20. Attach handles and tabs; mark design on tabs.
2. Embroider ovals and diamonds, using free motion zigzag stitch (pages 41-42). Work red ovals from edges toward centers; green diamonds in straight rows from side to side. **3.** Return machine to regular stitching and normal feed. With black, satin-stitch large scallops and outlines around other shapes.
4. Finish bag.

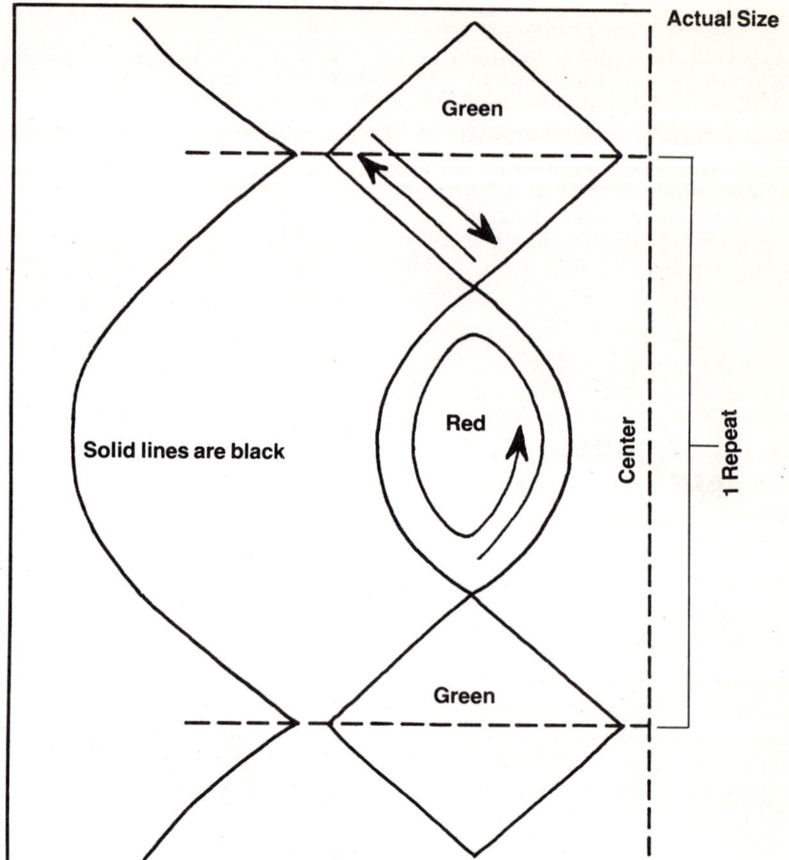

24/PUNCHWORK PILLOW ♥♥

Shown on page 40
Simplicity 7734

Materials: 75-yard (68.6 m) skeins of rug yarn, 1 each off-white, green and yellow, 2 red; monk's cloth or burlap; size 5 punch needle (1½″ or 3.8 cm from hole to hole); rug or stretcher frame; thumbtacks.

Directions (for finished size 14″ [35.5 cm] square): **1.** Cut fabric 2″ (5 cm) larger than finished size all around. Enlarge design, reverse and transfer to wrong side of fabric.
2. With design side up, stretch fabric on frame and tack edges in place.
3. Using punch needle as described on page 48, work design according to color chart, making stitches about ¼″ (6 mm) long and rows about ⅛ to 3/16″ (3 to 4.5 mm) apart.
4. Finish pillow.

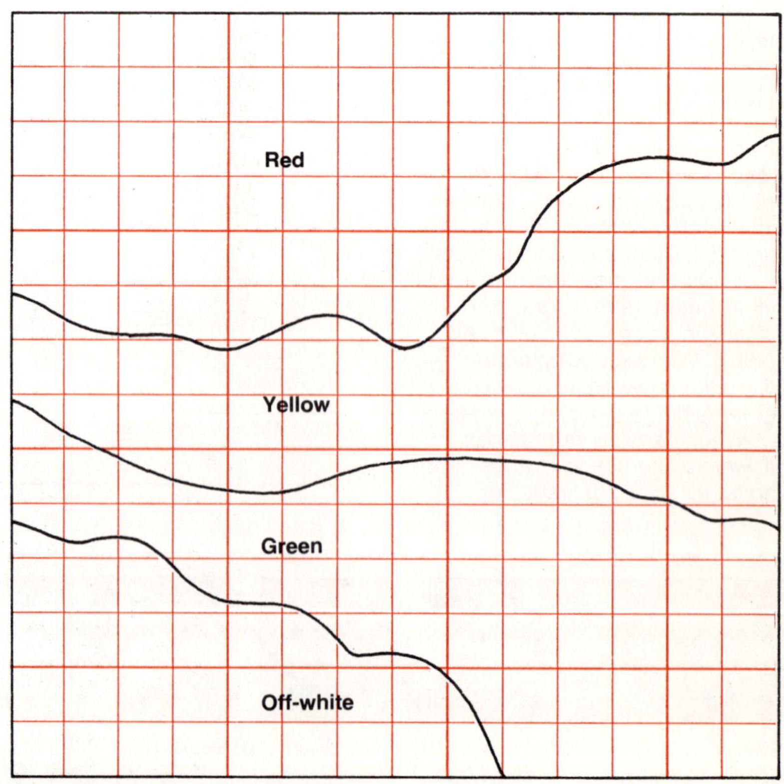

Scale: Each square = 1″ (2.5 cm)

With techniques geared to today's hectic schedules, decorative stitchery becomes a most effective way to Sew Something Special! Here are some nifty examples of fast stitchery for each category.

Trapunto sails prettily across an overall bib. Machine-stitched sailboat is stuffed and waves are corded for extra dimension. ♥♥

Textural interest defines this shapely obi belt. Machine-stitch a simple block design in large stitches and contrasting thread. ♥

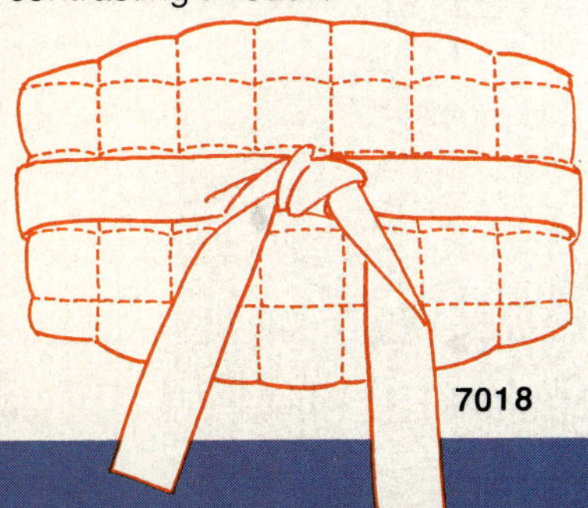

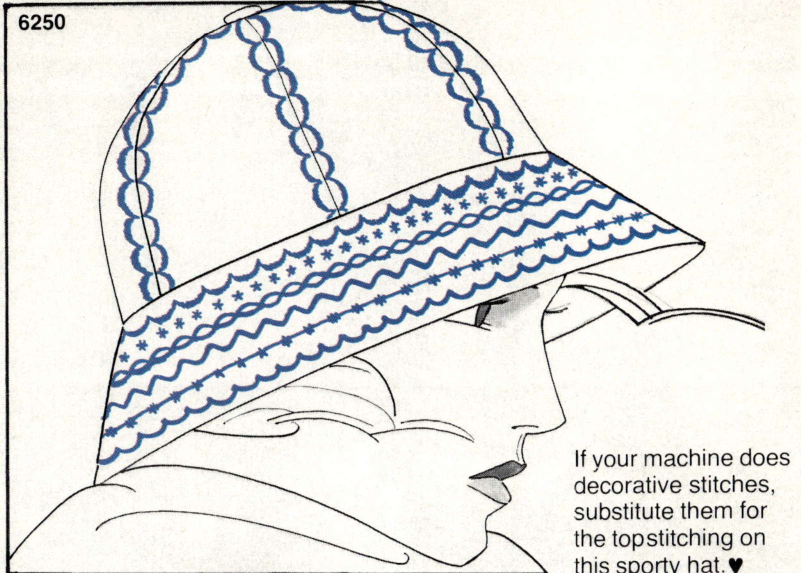

If your machine does decorative stitches, substitute them for the topstitching on this sporty hat. ♥

A soft blouson top is the perfect place to show off your embroidery know-how. Simply chain-stitch a "Fair Isle" design around neck. ♥♥

Needlepoint to wear—ours is a handsome vested version with fronts stitched up in a striking Bargello design. Easy to do. ♥♥

TERRIFIC TRIMS

GREAT DESIGNS

Trims are *in*, with a difference—as a design feature rather than an add-on! Use them to accent design lines . . . to create beautiful borders and textures.

25 Rows of soutache braid march up and down his shirt, creating a wealth of texture—all done easily with straight stitching.♥♥

26 Checked, dotted and striped ribbons weave a pretty design on her party-going tabard.♥

27 Bands of embroidered braid and ribbon arranged in square motifs make this table-topper something really special!♥

28 A lace doily is the inspiration for this serving tray, made from a handsome picture frame. Trims added to it create a nostalgic Victorian feeling.♥

29 A romantic pairing of lace and embroidered linen appliqués make this skirt and top the *most* fantastic dress-up ensemble!♥♥♥

For how-to's, see pages 67-68

7959

TERRIFIC TRIMS

Decorative as well as functional—that's the trim story right now! Here, casual outerwear sports trims used with imagination and flair.

30 Leg warmers get the treatment here, with lively embroidered ethnic-look trim forming the casings.♥♥

31 The basic duffle coat's not basic anymore! Not when you outline the simple shape with bright rickrack and add your own toggle closures made with foldover braid.♥♥

How-to's pages 67-68

TERRIFIC TRIMS

C

Make any fashion or accessory sparkle by trimming it. With all the imaginative trims available, trim departments are really fantasy lands—delightful places to browse in for inspiration. In fact, today's terrific trims are not just add-ons to a garment; often, they are what really *makes* the garment something special.

All the trim ideas in this chapter were selected for their ease and speed of application. Most can be applied by your sewing machine; some with the aid of a special presser foot. And, if you are really in a hurry, many can be fused, pressed or even glued on. Trimming can be a quick and easy way to sew creatively. Have fun!

TRIMMING HINTS

Here are some practical tips to help you with trims.

- When adding trim to a pattern that doesn't include it, first measure pattern or garment where trim is to be applied; buy at least ½ yard (.5 m) extra for joining ends and going around curves.
- Be sure the trim requires the same care as the fabric you're using.
- For curves, choose a flexible trim—rickrack, bias tape, narrow braid, foldover braid or knitted trim.
- When cutting trims, include a few extra inches (cm) for easing and finishing ends. Then, pin trim in place to check the finished effect.
- To hold trim in place, instead of pins, you could use double-faced basting tape, or iron it on with strips of fusible web before stitching.
- Stitch trims with a looser thread tension than normal, and ease them as you sew to avoid puckering.
- Unless trim is very narrow, miter corners of bands with a diagonal fold. Allow extra fullness to go around corners on ruffled edgings.
- Conceal trim ends at a side or back seam when possible. Otherwise, turn ends under and stitch across trim to secure.
- When layering several trims, such as bands and rickrack, stitch them together, then apply to garment.

The easy methods described here take so little time that you can spend a few minutes being extra-creative when sewing with trims.

APPLIQUÉ

Since appliqués come in all sizes, shapes and moods, look for one that suits you or combine several to achieve the look you want. Pin them on first to see if they work. Then follow instructions below to apply.

APPLYING

After pinning appliqué in place, edgestitch it with a straight or zigzag stitch (A). Or use fusible web cut to the appliqué shape and follow manufacturer's directions (B); edgestitch also, if desired.

A

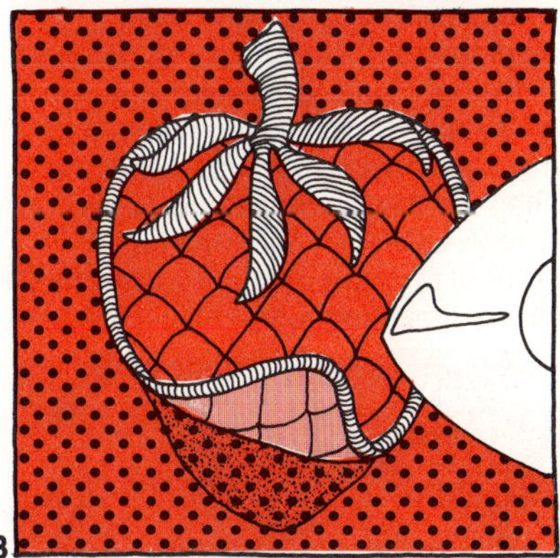

B

CREATIVE IDEAS

Your attic, antique store or a flea market may have treasures like lace handkerchiefs or doilies which make charming appliqués for tops, skirts or tablecloths (C). You can even make your own appliqués out of fabric scraps; see pages 19 and 20.

BINDING

Bindings serve two purposes: they conceal raw edges and trim the garment in one easy step. Use double-fold bias binding or foldover braid. Both have one side slightly wider for easy application.

APPLYING

For best results, pre-shape binding with a steam iron to match the shape of the garment edge. For an inward curve, stretch the two folded edges and press; for an outward curve, stretch the single folded edge (A).

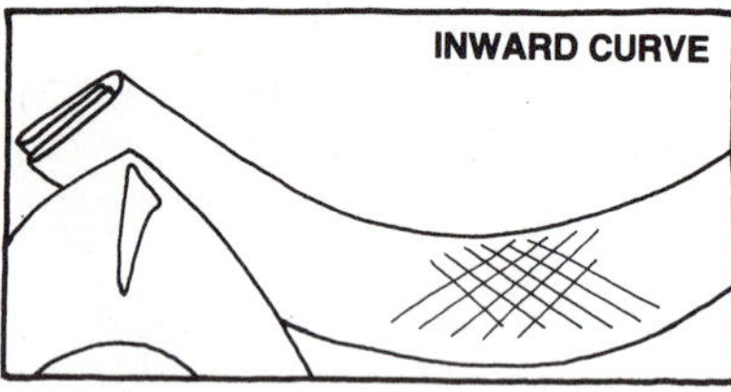

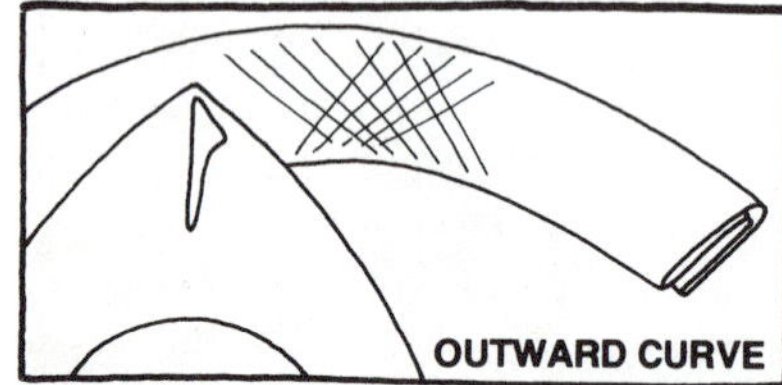

A

If you decide to bind an edge instead of facing it, you don't need to cut out the facings. Trim seam allowances from the edge to be bound; then, staystitch at a distance from the edge which corresponds to the width of the binding. Use this stitching as a guideline in keeping binding even.

Encase raw edges with binding, placing wider folded side on bottom. From right side, edgestitch through all layers. Some sewing machines have a binder foot which holds and attaches the binding at the same time (B). Check your machine manual for instructions on using this shortcut binding aid.

B

Inside Corners: Clip very carefully into corner edges, almost to stay-stitching. Encase one side of edge with binding, stitching to clip; leave needle in fabric. Pull corner so edge is straight (C), and continue stitching along second side of corner.
Fold out fullness on both sides of binding, forming a diagonally mitered corner; stitch folds (D).

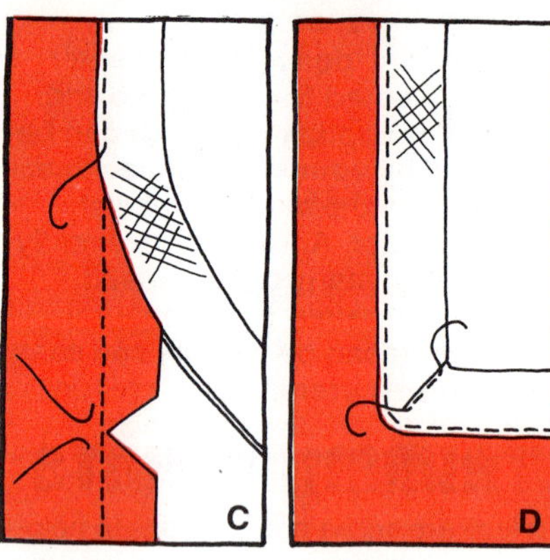

C D

Outer Corners: Bind one side of edge all the way to raw edge of corner (E); turn binding around corner and fold both sides diagonally to form a mitered corner; pin folds (F). Stitch second side, beginning at previous stitching.

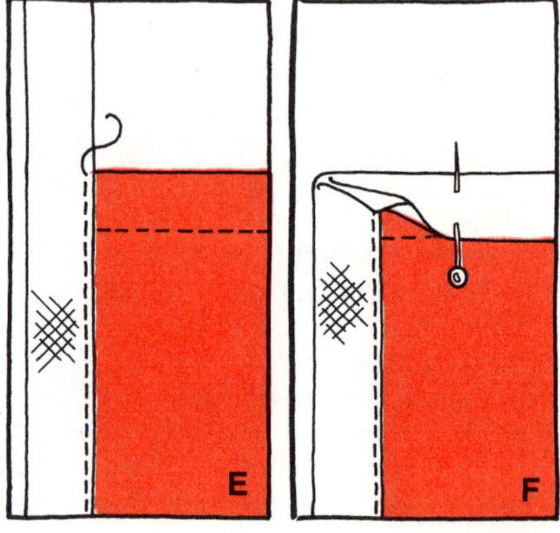

E F

BORDER OR TOP TRIM

Bands with straight or fancy edges can be used for borders or top trims, as can any trim with finished edges.

APPLYING WIDE TRIMS

Pin, fuse or tape trim. Topstitch along both edges of trim to edge of corner. To miter corner, fold trim back on itself and press. Fold trim diagonally at corner and press. Open fold and stitch along crease, through all layers (G). Continue to apply trim (H).

G

H

APPLYING NARROW TRIMS

Narrow, flat braid or yarn makes an interesting trim when applied with a straight or zigzag stitch. Pin or tape trim in place. Stitch through center or along both edges, depending on trim width. For very narrow braid or yarn, use a special-purpose braid foot with a groove that makes application easier and allows intricate curving designs. Hold fabric taut while stitching and ease trim to fabric (I).

Some narrow trims can be turned at a corner without mitering, while others must be mitered like wide trims.

I

CREATIVE IDEAS

Free Hanging Trims: Top trims are sometimes stitched on and several inches are left hanging free.

Before seaming garment, stitch a length of ribbon, banding or braid vertically or horizontally to the garment at the neck or shoulders, leaving a few inches free. Finish off the end by cutting diagonally, or add a bead and knot the end (A). You can also fringe the ends. Make a

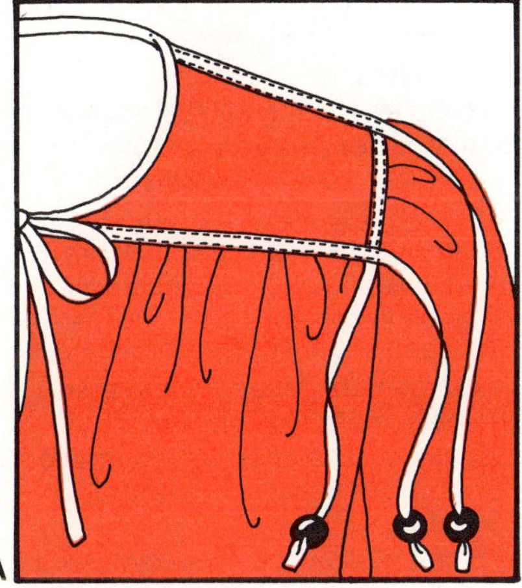
A

horizontal row of stitching as far away from the end as the length of fringe; pull horizontal threads away with a pin. Cut wider trim vertically to stitching at intervals to make pulling threads away easier (B).

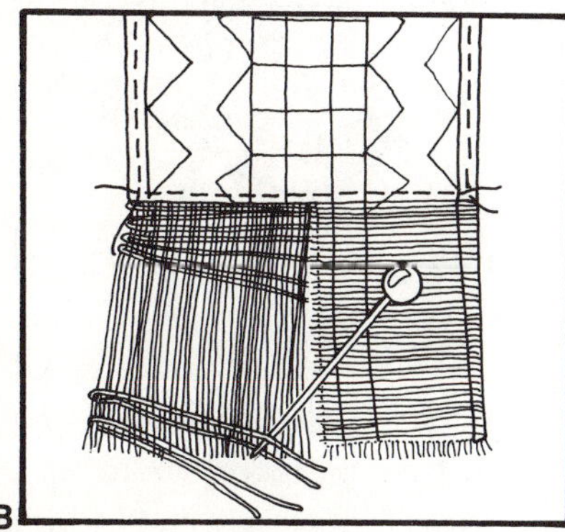
B

Applied Fringe: Although fringe is usually considered an edging, it can be used as a banding or border, topstitched a few inches in from garment edges. Sporty fringe can be cut from non-ravel fabrics, such as mock leather or suede, even felt. See Fringe, page 34. Or, make pretty knotted fringe of narrow satin or macrame cord and decorate the edges of shawls or evening bags.

Machine Couching: Zigzag-stitch over a narrow braid or yarn in matching or contrasting color thread. Zigzag stitches should be wide enough to pass over cord without stitching through it (C).

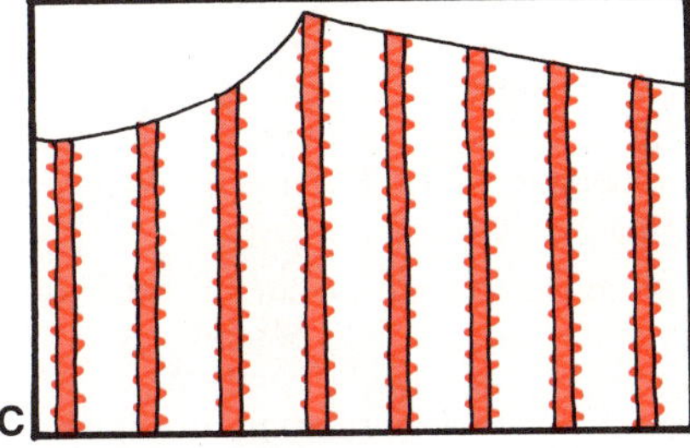
C

Bias Tape or Ribbons: Add a whole new dimension to fabric by crisscrossing ribbons or tape on a yoke or cuff for a checkered or woven effect. Simply run them along a hem edge for an effective border (D). Go the multi-stripe route with rows of banding. Mark position of trim on fabric. Measure and cut trim, including seam allowances. Use a decorative machine stitch along the edges for extra appeal. Strips of fusible web or basting tape will hold bands in place for stitching. Apply bands before garment sections are stitched together so ends can be caught in seams.

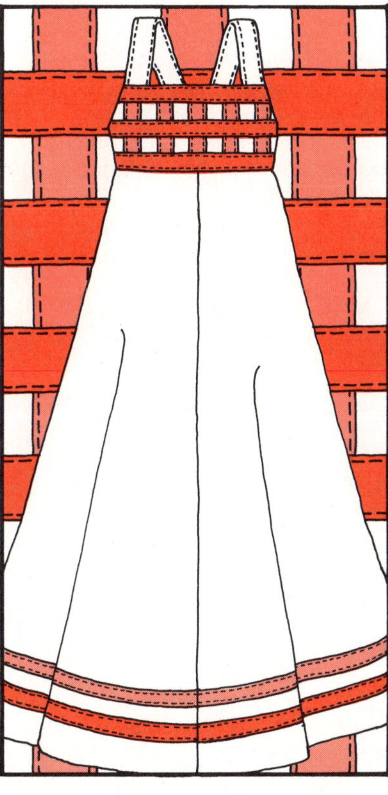
D

EDGING

Trims with at least one decorative edge, such as fringe, piping and pre-gathered ruffles, can make attractive edgings. They can be applied two ways.

INSERTED IN SEAM

Place trim on the right side of the fabric along the seam line with decorative edge toward garment (on pre-gathered ruffles,place bound edge inside seam line). Machine-baste the straight edge of trim (or middle of rickrack), following seam

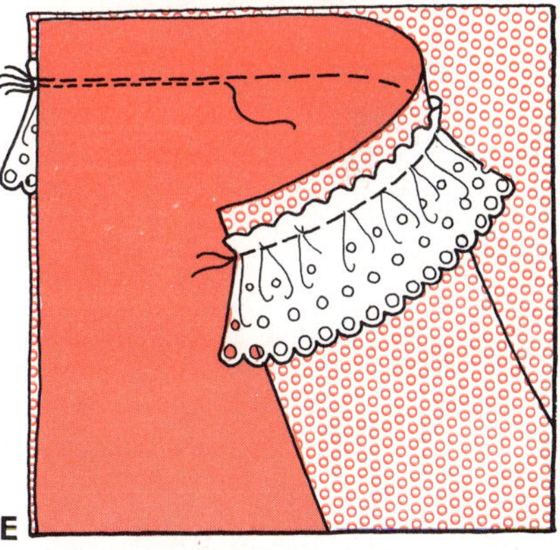
E

line. Pin garment sections together and stitch close to basting (E). Use a zipper foot to stitch piping or bound ruffles. Press seam allowances to one side.

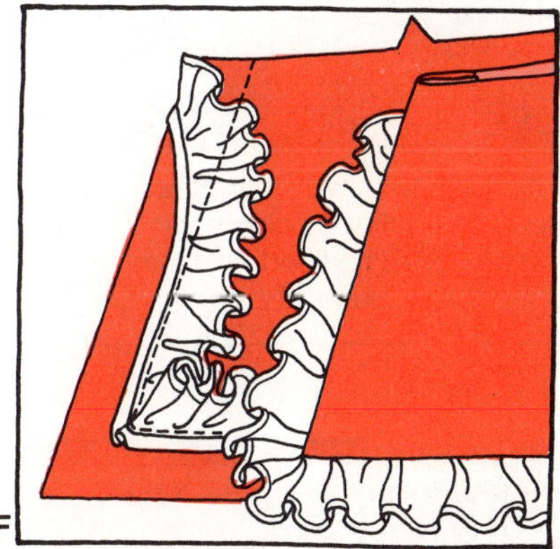
F

For ruffles and other pre-gathered trims on collars and cuffs, taper end of trim at edges which will be stitched to the garment. Allow extra fullness at corners by making a fold in trim. Then pin and stitch in place (F).

TOPSTITCHED ALONG EDGE

Lap finished garment edge (hem, pocket, collar, etc.) over straight edge of trim (on rickrack, lap so one set of points shows); topstitch close to garment edge (A). For piping, use a zipper foot to apply. To help guide stitching when applying edgings, use an edgestitcher foot (B).

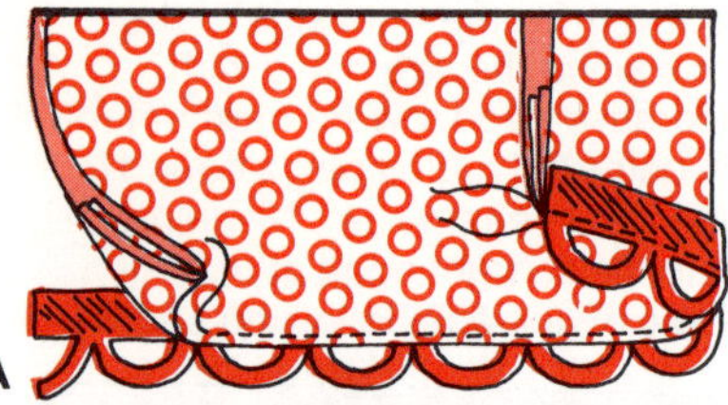

A

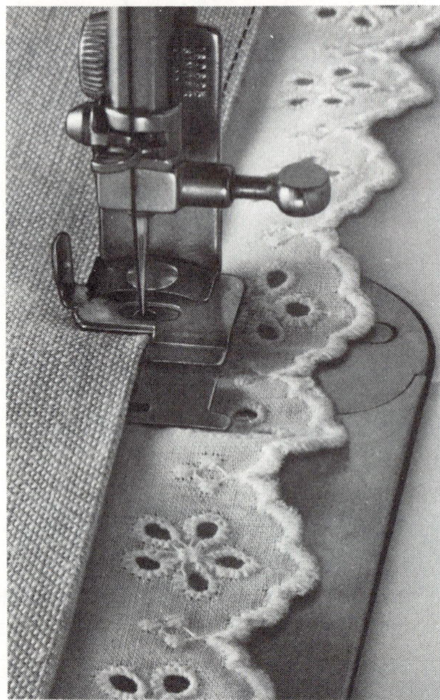

B

For trims with two finished edges, such as scalloped bands or rickrack, lap trim over finished fabric edge and topstitch in place (C).

C

INSERTION

See-through trims, such as lace or eyelet, with two finished edges are perfect for insertion. Inserts can be placed in flat garment areas, with no darts or curved seaming.

APPLYING

Apply insert on garment sections before seaming so ends of trim are included in seam. Pin trim in place and topstitch close to edges.

For scalloped edges, stitch a straight line just inside points of scallops leaving decorative edges free (D). At corners, miter insertion as shown on page 62. For the see-through effect, cut fabric from the wrong side

D

to within ¼″ (6 mm) of stitching. Press seam allowances away from trim and, from the right side, stitch over the first stitching (D). On fabrics that ravel, use a suitable seam finish. If you have an edgestitcher foot, you can join trim to fabric in one operation (E).

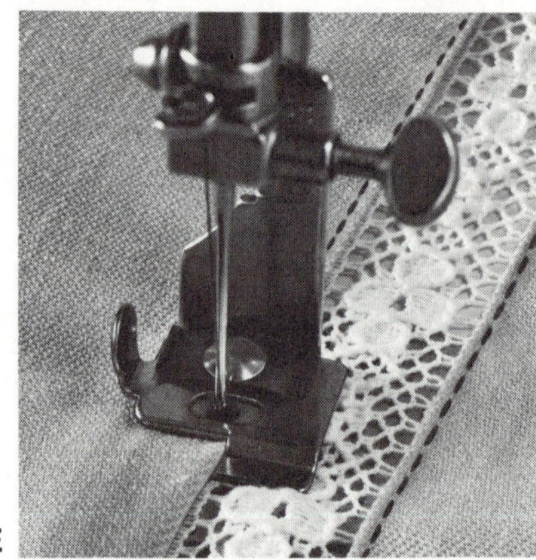

E

At seams, pin carefully with edges matching and stitch a regular seam; press open; stitch ¼″ (6 mm) from seam; trim insertion close to second stitching (F).

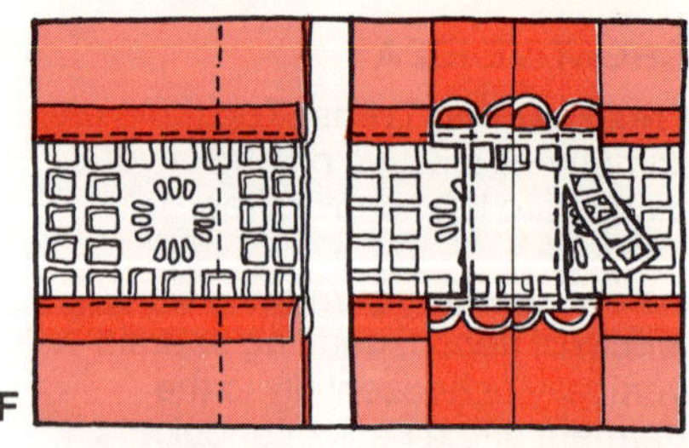

F

LACING

Certain types of trims, such as jute, leather, ribbon and cord, are great for decorative lace-ups.

APPLYING

Eyelets and lacing can be added to garments for closures and for decorative lacing—around armholes, the neck of a jumper, along a center front or side seam, even finishing off a hem edge. See page 69 for a neat skirt trick. The area should be interfaced for extra reinforcement. Measure and mark the placement of eyelets first. Usually, you can position them about ½″ (1.3 cm) from the edge and no further apart than ½″ or 1″ (1.3 or 2.5 cm). Follow the manufacturer's directions for applying eyelets. Then just thread the leather or cord in and out of the eyelets. Add a bead, if you wish, and knot each end to hold (G).

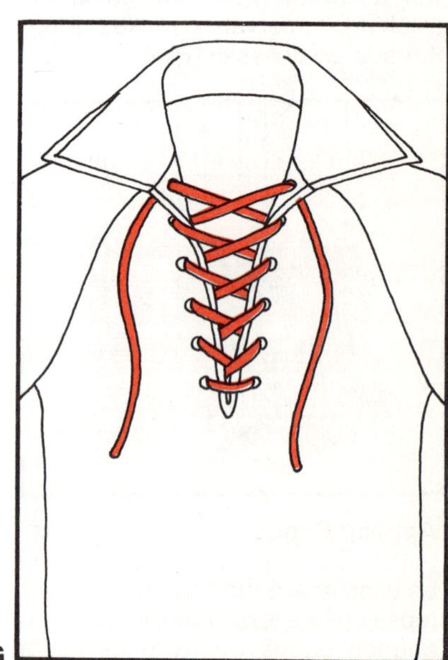

G

Some other good lacing materials are colored shoestrings, narrow ribbon or braid. Even cable cord, found in home decorating departments, makes nice lacing.

CREATIVE IDEAS
To make streamers, apply an eyelet to the fabric (on yoke, pocket, etc.), insert a narrow trim or leather strip and knot on the inside to hold. Add beads or small feathers at the dangling end and knot to secure.

You can use other lace-up devices. Decorative metal hooks that sew on make a good-looking closure (A). Or try rounded hooks, like those used on laced boots.

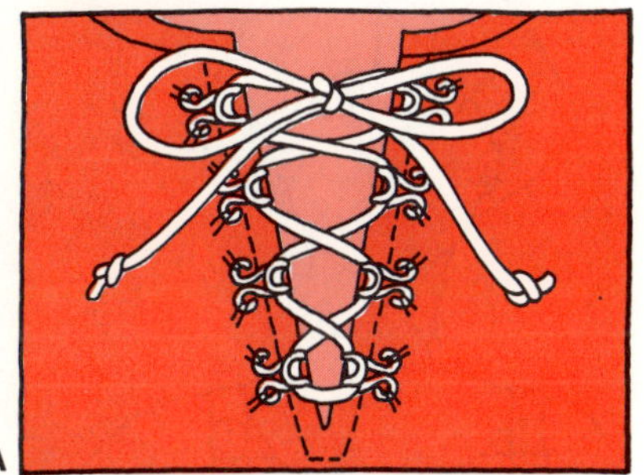

A

Make your own loops, using narrow ribbon or cording. Cut into 2″ (5 cm) strips and fold in half to form loops; machine-baste on right side along seam line, with folded edge of loops facing away from opening area (B). After facing is applied and pressed to inside, loops face toward opening (C). See page 34 for more lacing suggestions.

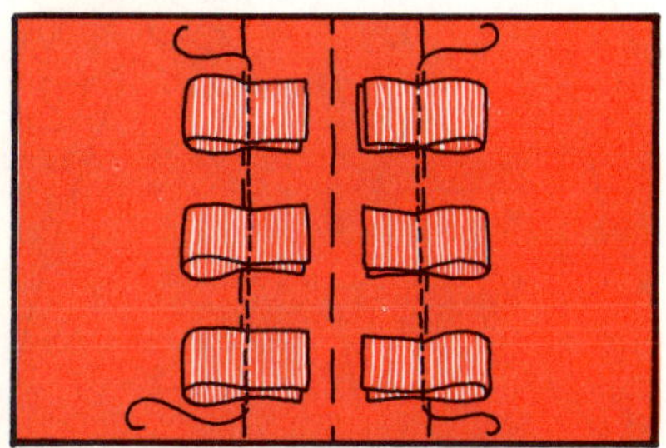

B

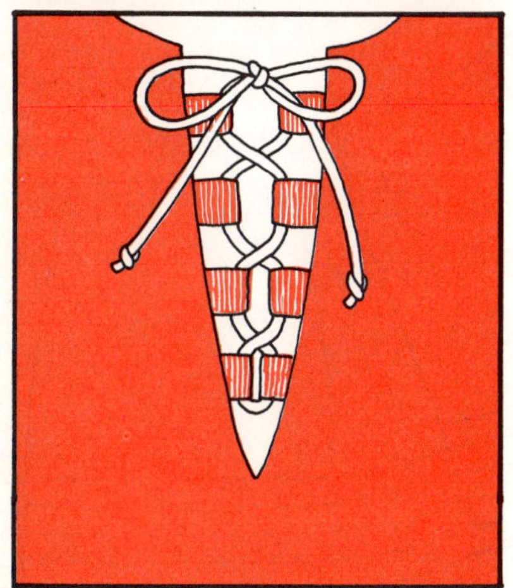

C

TRIM WEAVING

Many trims can be woven together to form marvelous fabrics to use in decorative ways. Almost any straight-edged trim will work—ribbons (grosgrain, velvet, satin, taffeta or embroidered), braids, leather strips, lace, or novelty bands.

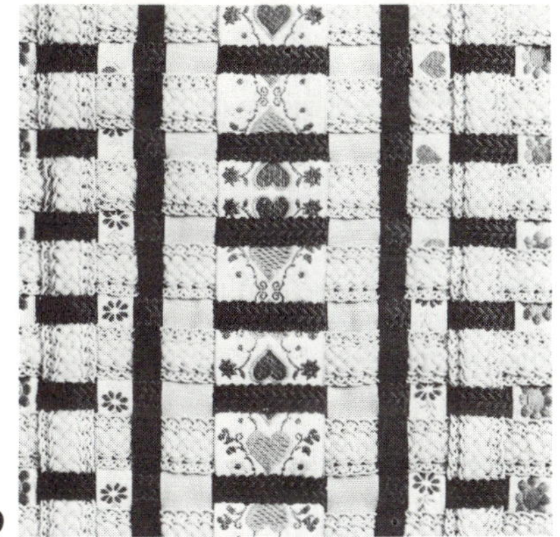

D

The same trim in two colors makes a graphic checkerboard design. Just one ribbon creates texture; an assortment of trims produces a rich tapestry of texture and colors (D). The backing can be covered, or you can have windows where the backing shows through, a charming way to use scraps of fabric. There are so many ways to use trim weavings that you will enjoy experimenting.

FIGURING YARDAGE
Ribbon: Plan your woven trim design on paper. Then figure how much trim in each color, laid side by side in strips, will cover the backing; add 1″ (2.5 cm) to each strip for finishing and *double* this to get the total amount. (Allow a little extra for trims that ravel easily). For example: If your ribbon is 1″ (2.5 cm) wide and your finished weaving will be 11″ x 11″ (27.9 x 27.9 cm), 11 pieces of ribbon 12″ (30.5 cm) long will cover the piece vertically. Another 11 pieces the same length are needed to cover it horizontally. If you are using two colors, you will need 11 pieces of each color, or 132″ or 3⅔ yards (3.40 m) of trim.

Backing: You'll need a backing to stabilize your weaving so it can be used as a fabric. Use muslin or broadcloth matching the color of the dominant trim. For an open-weave design, choose fabric to complement your design—velveteen, satin, or other contrasting textures. Buy enough fabric to back the finished weaving, plus ½″ (1.3 cm) seam allowances on all edges, or twice that amount for a pillow.

Whenever trim weaving is used in garments, simply cut the backing with your pattern or cut it to the size of the finished item, plus seam allowances on all edges.

Preparation: Preshrink all washable trims before cutting by immersing in a hot water bath for an hour.
Cut the backing to the finished weaving size, plus ½″ (1.3 cm) seam allowances. Cut trim into enough strips to cover the backing horizontally and vertically. Do not cover side seam allowances with vertical trim, or top and bottom seam allowances with horizontal trim (E).

WEAVING THE DESIGN
Line up trim strips vertically on backing. If you are planning to fuse trim, place web between backing and ribbon, now. Use T-pins or straight pins to anchor each strip in place at one end. Cover back except for seam allowances at either side. Anchor one end of the first horizontal trim ½″ (1.3 cm) from top of backing and weave it over and under the vertical strips (E). Repeat with remaining trims, keeping them as close together as possible.

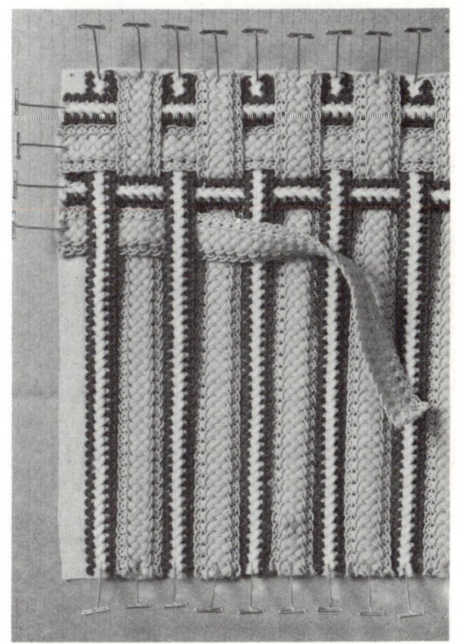

E

A

Fastening Weaving: Weaving can be secured to the backing by stitching, fusing or gluing. Stitching is preferred where the backing is covered entirely by trim. After weaving, pin and then machine-baste ends of trim to backing ½″ (1.3 cm) from edge around all sides (A). Keep ribbon edges butted together as you sew.

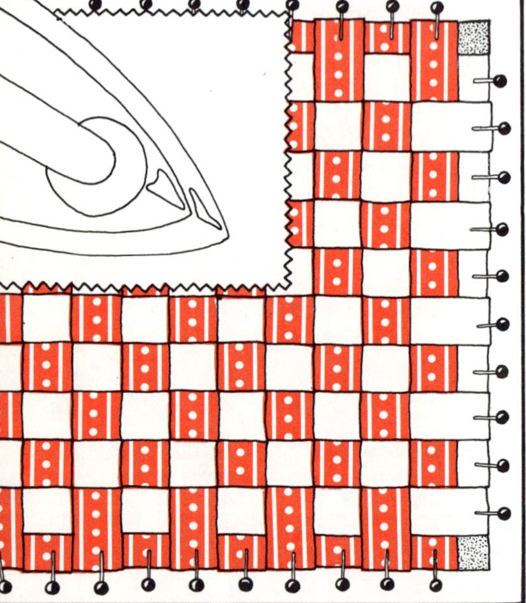

B

Fusible web can be used instead of stitching where the trim completely covers the backing. Cut web the same size as backing and place it over backing before weaving the design. After weaving, use steam iron and damp press cloth to fuse the three layers together carefully (B), following manufacturer's directions.

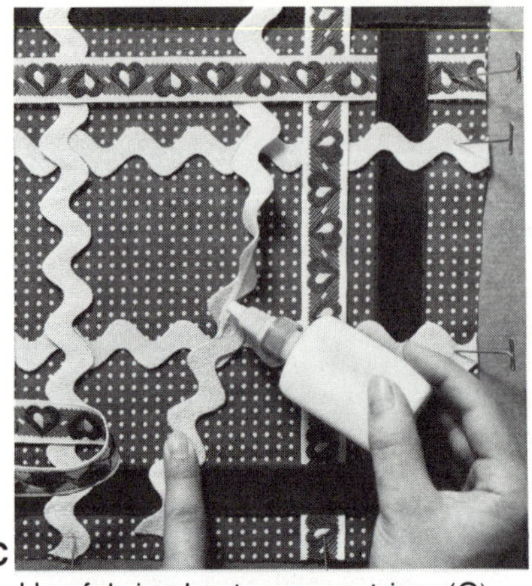

C

Use fabric glue to secure trims (C) where windows of backing show through or where trim design is loosely-woven.

CREATIVE IDEAS

Trim weavings make unusual and exciting home furnishings—pillows, table runners, book covers and placemats, as well as fashion accessories like evening bags, belts or tote bags. Their effect can be formal or casual, depending on the trims you choose.

Trim weaving is equally versatile on collars, cuffs, pockets and yokes (D).

D

PROJECT INSTRUCTIONS

25/MAN'S CAFTAN TOP♥♥

Shown on page 58
Simplicity 7441, View 1

Materials for size 40: 16 yds. (14.65 m) soutache braid.

Directions: 1. Cut out top; pencil-mark point of neckline slash and center front line. For braid placement, mark 4 parallel vertical lines on each side of front, starting 1½" (3.8 cm) from center front, with each 1½" (3.8 cm) apart. Mark right, then left side. **2.** Sew braid in place, starting at hem edge and extending ½" (1.3 cm) into neckline and shoulder seam allowances. **3.** To make guide for rest of braid placement, cut out 3" (7.6 cm) square of paper; fold twice

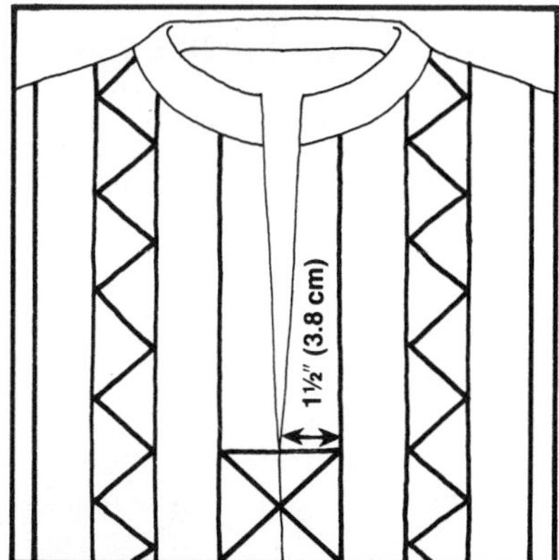

diagonally to form an X. **4.** Using this guide, mark horizontal line ¼" (6 mm) below slash point. Lay one edge of guide on this line; re-fold along diagonal lines and mark first X. Continue marking X's down to hem. For side front zigzag lines and border at sleeve edge, fold X-guide into triangular quarters; use triangle to mark position lines. **5.** Measure length of braid for center front design; place center ¼" (6 mm) below slash point and stitch horizontal line . Then stitch braid down front, and on side front design, extending it into neckline seam allowance. **6.** Finish top except sleeves. Sew braid to collar seam; turn under ¼" (6 mm) at opening. **7.** Stitch braid to sleeve hem edge as on front. Finish garment.

26/TABARD WITH RIBBONS♥

Shown on page 58
Simplicity 8165

Materials (for size 10): ¾" (2 cm) wide fusible web strips; ribbons in variety of designs and widths, in these amounts: ½, 1, 1 and 1½ yds. (0.50, 0.95, 1.40 m) of four different ⅞" (2.2 cm) width, 1 yd. (0.95 m) 1" (2.5 cm) width, 1 yd. (0.95 m) 1½" (3.8 cm) width, ½ yd. (0.50 m) 2⅛" (5.3 cm) width, ⅝ yd. (0.60 m) 2⅝" (6.5 cm) width.

Directions: Complete tabard. Use ribbon widths in diagram below as guide to place ribbons on tabard front or follow photo on page 58. Fuse-baste ribbons in place, fusing first those with raw ends covered by other ribbons. At side, neckline, shoulder seams and X's, turn ends under; edgestitch.

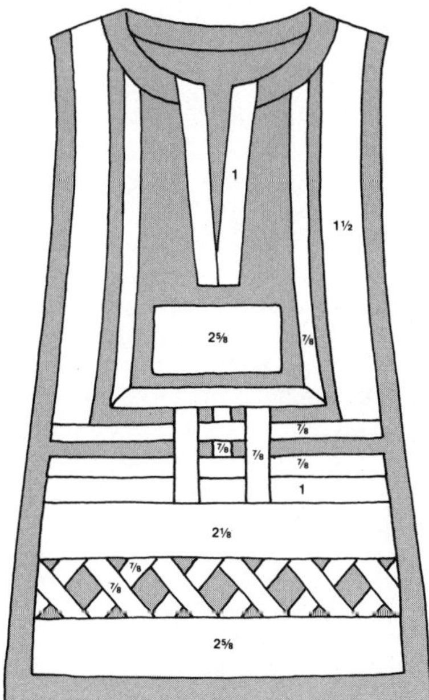

27/SQUARE TABLE TOPPER♥

Shown on pages 58-59

Materials for finished size about 33" (84 cm) square with edging: 1 yd. (.95 m) glazed cotton, 4¼ yds. (3.90 m) of 2" (5 cm) floral banding for A, 2½ yds. (2.30 m) of ⅝" (1.5 cm) grosgrain ribbon for B, 1¼ yds. (1.15 m) of 1¼" (3.2 cm) crochet-type lace banding for C, 3¾ yds. (3.45 m) of 1" (2.5 cm) lace edging for D.

Diagram 1

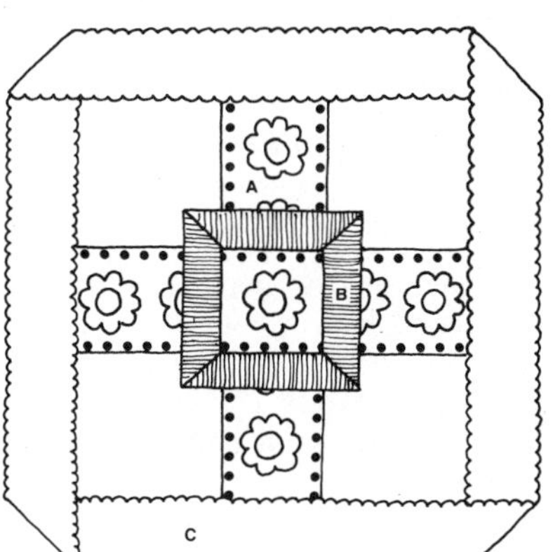

Diagram 2

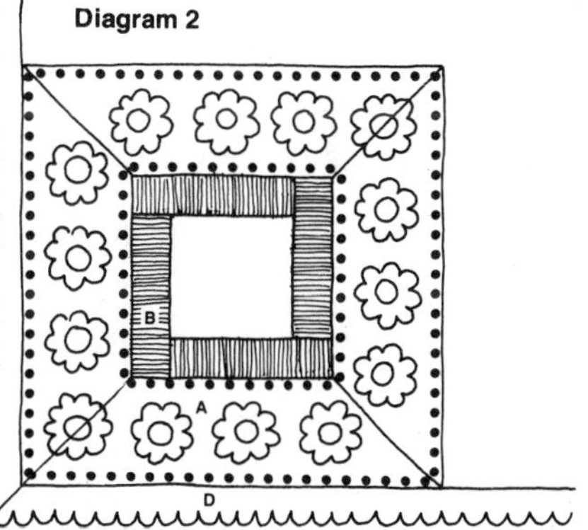

Directions: 1. Cut fabric 34" (86.6 cm) square. Fold edges under ½" (1.3 cm) twice; press and stitch. **2.** Fold square in half both ways to find center; mark. **3.** For center (Diagram 1), cut two 7½" (19.3 cm) strips of A; mark centers on wrong sides. Pin one strip across cloth at center, matching centers; edgestitch. Pin second strip crossing the first, matching centers; edgestitch. Cut 14" (35.5 cm) length of B. Pin B where A's intersect, forming square with mitered corners. Trim excess B and conceal end under fold; edgestitch. Pin C around outside, covering A ends, to form square as shown; trim excess C and conceal end under first corner; stitch. **4.** For each corner (Diagram 2), cut 33" (84 cm) length of A. Pin to corner in an 8" (20.5 cm) open square with mitered corners and two sides along corner hem; edgestitch outside edges of square only. Cut four 4½" (11.5 cm) strips of B; pin strips inside A square, with corners overlapping, edges touching A and ends slipped under A; stitch both edges and remaining A edge. **5.** For edging, lap one edge of D ½" (1.3 cm) over hem, miter corners, and stitch all around.

28/SERVING TRAY♥

Shown on page 58

Materials: Tray was 20 x 14″ (51 x 35.5 cm), made from a picture frame with glass and drawer-pull handles. Velvet to cover backing, 9¾″ (25 cm) doily, 1½ yds. (1.40 m) 1″ (2.5 cm) wide edging (A), 1⅞ yds. (1.75 m) ½″ (1.3 cm) braid (B), 1¼ yds. (1.15 m) 1″ (2.5 cm) wide double ruffling (C), 4 yds. (3.70 m) ¼″ (6 mm) wide ribbon (D), 1½ yds. (1.40 m) ½″ (1.3 cm) wide lace (E), fabric glue.
Directions: Glue velvet to backing. Place all trims over velvet as shown. Glue in place. Reassemble tray.

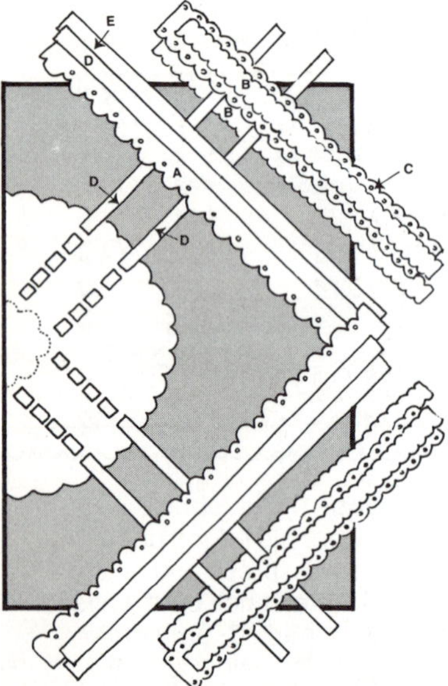

29/TOP AND SKIRT WITH LACE TRIM♥♥♥

Shown on page 59
Simplicity 7959

Materials: Tablecloth or placemats with at least 5 embroidered or appliquéd motifs and embroidered edges (3 for top, 2 for skirt), each about 10½ x 7″ (26.8 x 18 cm); 6 smaller corner motifs from napkins or bun warmers for skirt; ½ yd. (0.50 m) stretch lace, 2½ yds. (2.30 m) ¾″ (2 cm) width satin ribbon; four 1¼″ (3.2 cm) width lace trims—3¼ yds. (3.00 m) A, 4 yds. (3.70 m) B, 3¼ yds. (3.00 m) C, 2 yds. (1.85 m) D.

Directions: 1. Assemble top up to Unit 2, using lace instead of braid. Do not slipstitch shoulders yet. Cut motif with embroidered edge from tablecloth 6½″ (16.3 cm) wide in a triangular shape. Press under raw edges ¼″ (6 mm). Center motif on top front with finished edge at neckline. Pin; edgestitch folds. Cut away fabric and lace under motif ¼″ (6 mm) from stitching; press. **2.** Finish sleeve hem. Cut two rectangular motifs with finished edges 7″ (18 cm) wide and to fit height of sleeve; press sides under ¼″ (6 mm). Center motif on sleeve, finished edge at hem; edgestitch sides. Baste top of motif along sleeve cap; trim motif even with sleeve. Cut away sleeve fabric under motif ¼″ (6 mm) from stitching. Repeat for other sleeve. Finish top. **3.** Cut out skirt, omitting pockets and drawstring. Sew center front and back seams; press open. **4.** Make pieces 1 and 20 from plain tablecloth area. For #1, cut rectangle 8 x 14″ (20.5 x 35.5 cm); make five ⅜″ (1 cm) deep tucks ¾″ (2 cm) apart, parallel to short edge; topstitch in place with two rows of stitching. Cut piece into a diamond 4″ (10 cm) on each side, with horizontal tucks; cut in half vertically. For #20, cut a rectangle 8 x 10″ (20.5 x 25.5 cm). Cut lace C into five 10″ (25.5 cm) strips; sew one strip to each long fabric edge. Sew on other strips as insertions (page 64) 1¼″ (3.2 cm) apart. Cut rectangle in half crosswise; turn raw edges under ½″ (1.3 cm) and press. **5.** Enlarge diagram to fit skirt front. Use diagram to cut pieces: #4 from tablecloth motif; 3, 5 and 6 from corner motifs; and the lace according to diagram. **6.** Place diagram over skirt right front and pin. Slip #'s 1-12 under tracing and pin (slip ends of 9, 10 under 7; 11, 12 under 9, 10). Remove diagram; edgestitch lace. Replace diagram; and place and stitch #'s 13-18 and then #'s 19-22. **7.** Do left front same way. **8.** Assemble skirt; add satin ribbon drawstring.

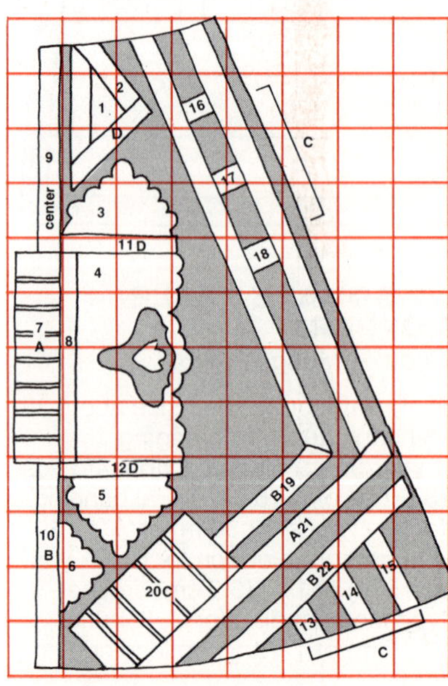

Scale: Each square = 2¾″ (7 cm)

30/LEG WARMERS♥♥

Shown on page 60
Simplicity 8146

Materials: 4 yds. (3.70 m) 1″ (2.5 cm) banding, 8 yds. (7.35 m) cord.

Directions: 1. Cut out leg warmers. Mark casing lines on outside; stitch back seams. **2.** Cut banding so ends can be turned under ½″ (1.3 cm) and edgestitch along casing lines, turning ends under. Finish leg warmers. **3.** Cut cord into 8 lengths, draw through casings; knot ends.

31/HOODED JACKET♥♥

Shown on page 60
Simplicity 7936, View 2

Materials: Foldover braid in pattern yardage plus 45″ (115 cm), narrow rickrack—7⅜ yds. (6.75 m) for size 10, 45″ (115 cm) seam tape, fusible web strips, 6 toggle buttons.

Directions: 1. Make jacket, omitting closing snaps; sew rickrack on pockets and along edges of jacket and hood, near braid. **2.** Cut extra braid into three 15″ (38 cm) strips. Insert seam tape inside braid and fuse all layers together. Butt ends of each strip and tack together. Fold braid loops into mitered points, positioning ends of braid near one end of mitered point as shown;

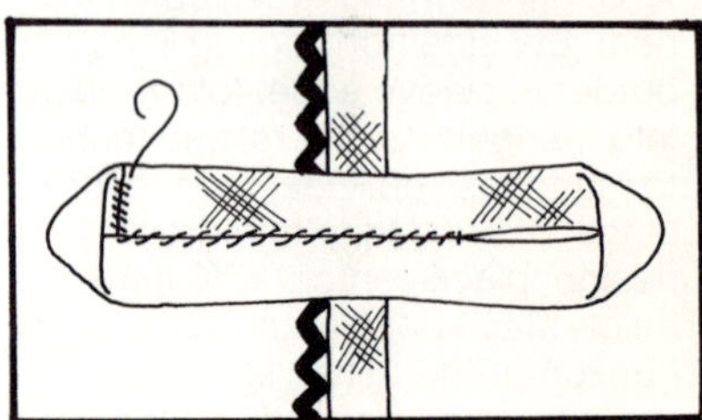

press. Slipstitch centers together, leaving opening at one end for toggles as shown. Pin first fastener 1″ (2.5 cm) from rickrack at top of right front, with center at jacket center front. Pin others below, 3″ (7.6 cm) apart; slipstitch. Sew toggles on left and right front.

Imaginative trimmings add style, dimension and originality to your sewing. Updated methods help you stitch, glue and fuse your way to especially creative fashions, gifts and home furnishings.

Fuse bias strips and ribbons to fabric to create a colorful geometric wall hanging.♥

Make a patchwork wreath from old ties, velvet or satin. Tie each section with narrow trim.♥

Romantic pillow is made by stitching on a doily appliqué before assembling. Lace edging completes the theme.♥

Pretty peasant blouse shows off topstitched ribbon streamers with beads knotted at ends. Ribbons tie up neck and sleeves, too.♥

Then, lace a ribbon through eyelets, applied along the center front of a basic skirt, for the perfect partner.♥

More peasantry . . . via decorative braid topstitched along seams of the completed dress. For a great finish, the braid-trimmed belt.♥

ADD A CRAFT

FUN FOR ALL TO DO

Go one step beyond stitching—Add A Craft. Each of these clever projects combines sewing with a craft technique that's easy and fun to do. There's something for everyone!

32 Stitched-and-stuffed pillows tied together in a row make lying down a dreamy experience. Relax in style, outdoors or in.♥♥

33 All those odd buttons you've been saving for years are right at home on this button-bedecked vest. Sew them on with contrasting embroidery floss.♥♥♥

34 Jaunty knotted fringe dangles from a petite shoulder purse. Tie a few simple knots for the dangles, then braid some cord for the strap, and you've got it made.♥

35 A flirty knitted ruffle runs 'round this comfy pillow—a simple mock-ribbing stitch makes it easy.♥

36 Scenic collage borrows textures from nature, with a little help from your collection of fabrics and sewing basket whatnots.♥♥

37 Easy-to-knit sleeves and pockets add a dash of texture and warmth to his sporty-looking jacket.♥♥

38 Multi-textured yarns braided together (what could be simpler?) form closures while adding an ethnic flavor to a basic jacket.♥

39 Super-shaggy yarn texture gives a hand-loomed feeling to this naturalistic rug. Just latch-hook a few areas here and there on loosely-woven, sturdy fabric.♥♥♥

See pages 79-80 for all how to's

7253
7614

ADD A CRAFT

Sewing and crafts use lots of creative materials—yarns, fabrics, ribbon, cord —and many crafty routes from knitting and crochet to stitch-and-stuff! Here, more crafty projects!

40 Whimsical stuffed mushrooms are stitched up in a subtle mix of fabrics for a great pillow group.♥♥

8121

41 A favorite stuffed animal inspired the knit pocket added to her sweatshirt. The fringy tail and mane make it extra fun!♥

42 For the romantic camisole, crochet a dainty ruffled edging; lace with ribbon.♥♥♥

8072

Instructions, pages 79-80

ADD A CRAFT

Sewing and crafts naturally complement each other. Even though your trusty sewing machine is a creative tool by itself, why stop at sewing when you can add a fabulous one-of-a-kind finish with crochet or knitting? Or, perhaps you will enjoy turning sewing into a craft with stitch-and-stuff techniques or collage. Some crafts not traditionally associated with sewing are especially creative. Did you know, for example, that you can combine knotting or braiding with sewing for an unusual decorative touch? You'll discover many more beautiful ways that sewing and crafts go together in this chapter.

A

STITCH & STUFF

With stitch-and-stuff methods, you can create simple three-dimensional objects, like pillows, toys and dolls. Or you can do soft sculpture, a new art form that's nothing more than imaginative stitched-and-stuffed shapes used in novel ways, like wall hangings or fabric sculptures (A). Use Simplicity patterns for many stitch-and-stuff projects, or design your own; see pages 5 and 70 for ideas. Just be sure to choose simple shapes for your first project—a cactus, the moon, stars or hearts.

FABRICS

Firmly-woven fabrics that do not ravel easily are best. Felt is an excellent choice, since it's sturdy and needs no seam finishing. Stable, slightly stretchy double-knits mold well around stuffing. Some fabrics can imitate nature—satin for leaves or water, tweed or a print for earth and rocks, and fake fur for shaggy animals or corduroy, velveteen and terry for short-hairs.

CUTTING AND ASSEMBLING

For your own designs, lay out and cut pieces double, adding ¼" (6 mm) seam allowances. Mark all the details—darts, tucks and trim placement. If possible, add some decorative touches like painting or embroidery before assembling. Embroider sections too small for a hoop before cutting out. On toys, you might use a button fastener to attach buttons securely. Stitch seams with strong thread and 12 to 15 stitches per inch (2.5 cm), reinforcing corners and sharp curves by stitching twice, and leaving openings for turning. Clip curves and press seams.

Choose a stuffing that suits the project. For pillows and cushions, buy standard-size pillow forms or cut sheets of foam to size with a serrated knife or sharp shears. Stuff irregular shapes with shredded foam, fiberfill or old nylons cut into strips. Use enough stuffing to define the shape smoothly; you'll find the eraser end of a pencil helpful in stuffing narrow areas.

Close openings by slipstitching. Add any decoration—painting or embroidery—not already done; on toys, attach buttons or beads securely to keep small fingers from prying them off.

BRAIDING AND KNOTTING

It's natural to talk about braiding and knotting together since both are made by interlocking strands of yarn, cord or similar materials. They make beautiful trims, straps, handles, closures or belts. See our jacket with braided yarn closures, page 71.

MATERIALS

You can do most braiding and knotting with various interesting materials—textured yarns, string or twine, satin or macramé cord. And don't overlook suede and leather strips, available by the yard. Just imagine sportswear or outerwear trimmed with suede or leather braids or fringe! You can also braid ribbon and packaged double-fold bias binding, saving you the trouble of cutting and folding fabric strips. And you can tie on beads, shells or other baubles by knotting the ends below them. You can estimate the amount of braiding material to buy by allowing a little over three times the length of the finished braid, including seam allowances for both ends. For knotted fringe you make yourself, multiply number of strands by the length of the unknotted strand, including seam allowances.

MAKING THE BRAID

Braids can dress up a head wrap, pants or a skirt (A). To make a long braid, tie the ends to a stationary object (doorknob, desk drawer) and keep the braid taut as you work. After braid is complete, stitch across the ends. Or, knot the ends together and leave long strands for tie closures or belts; then add wooden beads and knot ends or fluff ends with a pin (see page 63).

A

When braiding bias binding, keep the folded edge facing in the same direction to produce a uniform, flat braid. To attach the braid as a trim, sew it on by hand, concealing stitches underneath the braid and turning the ends under, or catch ends in a seam. To use as a strap or tie, catch the ends of the braid in a seam, or place them behind the fabric edge and topstitch.

Creative Ideas: Place flat braids made of ribbon or bias tape side by side, or coiled, and zigzag the edges of the braids together (B). Use "fabric" you've formed this way to make placemats (see page 81), pillows or an unusual tote bag (why not add braided handles).

B

KNOTTING AND FRINGE

To do knotting on a project, you'll need to insert individual strands or purchased fringe in a seam. Knotted fringe is an effective edge finish for a shawl, pillow, coverlet or wall hanging. It can also be an important design feature of a garment. For the strands, you can use long purchased fringe or cut your own. Just wind yarn around cardboard half as wide as fringe length; cut at edge. Strands may be spaced close together, in groups, or at intervals. You may also vary the lengths of groups of strands. Cut strands ⅝" (1.5 cm) longer than finished length.

To sew strands or fringe into seams or faced edges, place strands one next to the other or spaced at intervals on the right side of fabric section, ends even with the edge; hold in place with tape on the seam allowance. Seam or face as usual, catching ends in the stitching (C). Or tape strands of fringe to the underside of a finished hem and double-topstitch to hold in place (D). Then, knot one strand or knot two together. Better yet, add a small bead before knotting.

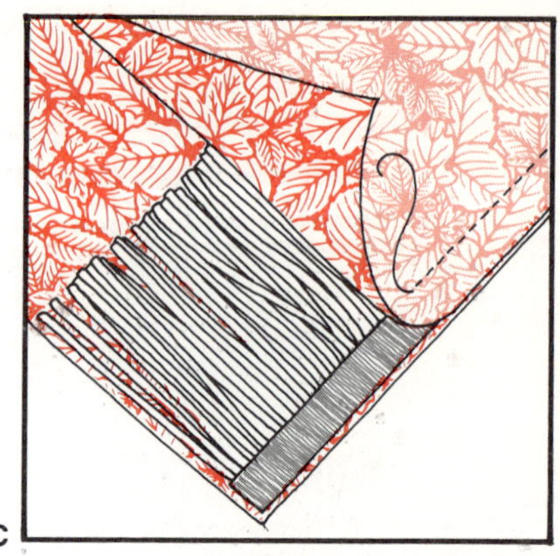

C

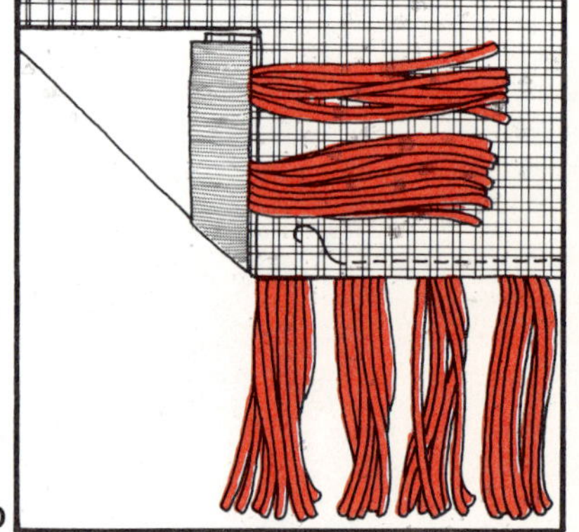

D

Creative Ideas: Tie grouped strands of yarn or cord about 8" (20 cm) or longer into lattice fringe for a luxurious effect that's simple to do. Divide strands into groups of the same number. Starting at one end, knot first group of strands to half the strands in second group. Continue across, knotting half the strands in one group to half the strands in the next (E). Tie two or three rows, leaving long ends. Trim ends. Try this on an evening bag (page 70).

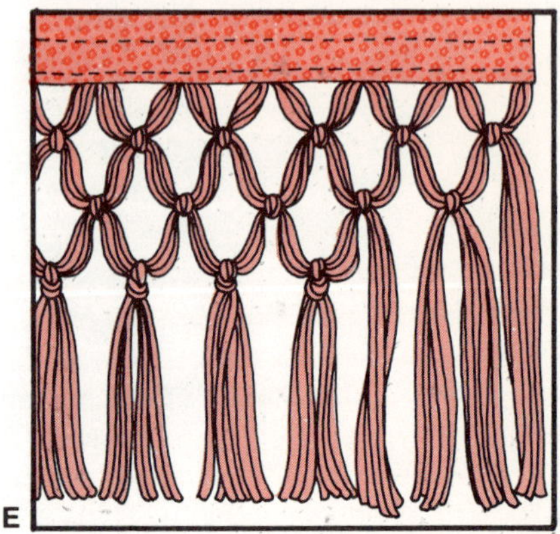

E

HOOKING

No doubt you've seen—perhaps even worked—a latch-hook rug on canvas. The same technique can be used to give a shaggy, hand-loomed feeling to fabric. Just select a nubby fabric or bedspread with a loose weave and an interesting design, such as bands or stripes; then highlight some areas with hooked-on shag. Your newly-textured fabric can make a really original rug, carryall, bedspread, afghan or wall hanging in just a fraction of the time required for a hand-loomed article.

MATERIALS

Hooking can be done on burlap, monk's cloth, heavy homespun or any other loosely-woven fabric that will support the knots of yarn. Just be sure the latch hook slips through the weave easily. Cut fabric 1″ (2.5 cm) larger all around than desired finished size. To keep edges from fraying as you work, turn the margin under and apply sew-on or iron-on rug binding. You can buy precut rug yarn in 2½″ (6.3 cm) lengths, or cut your own strands any length you prefer. Just wind yarn around cardboard half as wide as strand length; cut at edge.

LATCH HOOKING

To work, fold a strand of yarn around shank of latch hook, yarn ends even. Beginning at lower corner, insert hook under a horizontal thread of fabric until the latch appears (A). With latch open, wrap yarn to the left under hook. Close latch and pull hook back under horizontal thread, forming a knot (B). Tighten by pulling ends. Continue to form knots across the fabric, spacing them as desired. For dense shag, place knots close together. Uneven lengths, different yarns and random spacing make interesting textural effects.

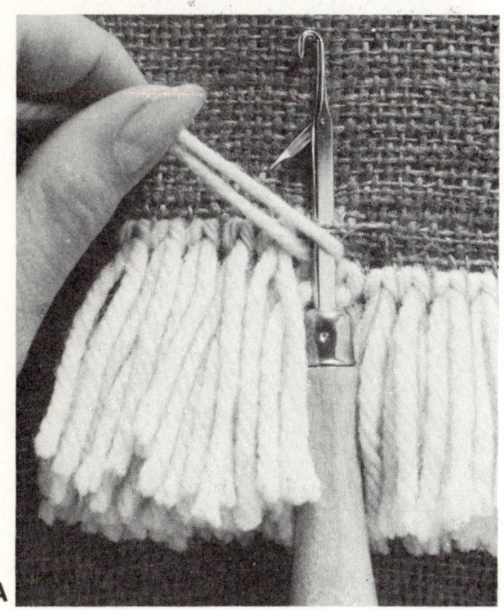

A

B

CROCHET

A delightful craft that runs the gamut from delicate lace to bold textured rugs, crochet allows a tremendous range of creative fashion and home furnishing possibilities. All you need is a knowledge of simple crochet stitches.

ABBREVIATIONS

ch—chain
st(s)—stitch(es)
sc—single crochet
dc—double crochet
hdc—half double crochet
tr—treble
sl st—slip stitch

EDGINGS

Dresses, blouses, T-shirts and lingerie all benefit from the charming addition of crocheted edgings (C). Let the fashion fabric and style of the garment determine the material for the edging—fine crochet cotton for lightweight fabric, medium-weight yarn for heavier fabric.

Before you begin the edging, hem or face edges in the usual way. Then, with an adjustable hole puncher, make small holes in dense fabrics ⅛″ (3 mm) from edge, ⅛ to ¼″ (3 to 6 mm) apart. Make size of holes compatible with yarn you will use. Some loosely-woven fabrics will not require pre-punching, as the hook will easily go through the weave. Here are two simple, versatile edgings. We used a standard crochet cotton and a #7 steel crochet hook.

C

Picot Edging: Work a row of sc through holes in fabric; ch 1, turn. **Row 2:** Sc in first sc, * ch 4, sl st in 2nd ch from hook (to form picot), ch 2, skip 2 sc, sc in next sc; repeat from * along garment edge (C, D).

D

Shell Edging: On wrong side, work a row of sc through holes in fabric; ch 1, turn. **Row 2:** Sc in first sc, * ch 1, skip 1 sc, 3 dc in next sc, ch 1, skip 1 sc, sc in next sc; repeat from * along edge (E).

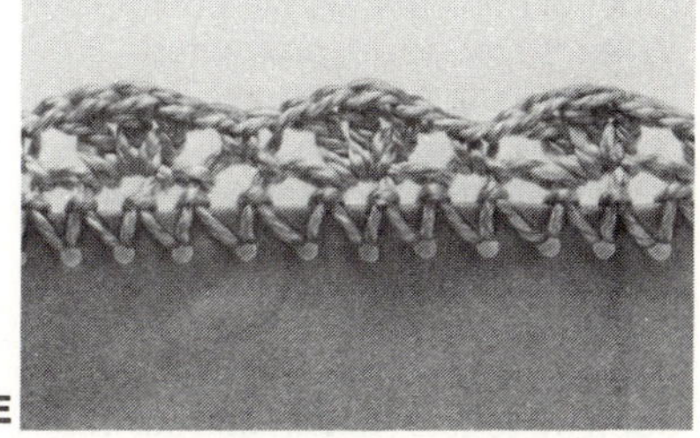

E

RUFFLES

Crochet can also be used to create ruffles. The one we show is worked flat (A); it is then gathered up by machine. For this ruffle, we used standard crochet cotton and a #7 steel crochet hook. Measure the edge where ruffle is to be attached, then plan to make the ruffle about twice as long to allow for fullness.

Lacy Ruffle: Ch a multiple of 10 sts to measure 2 to 2½ times the length of the edge. **Row 1:** Dc in 3rd ch from hook, dc in each ch across; ch 4, turn (multiple of 5 dc plus 3). **Row 2:** Tr in 2nd and 3rd dc, ch 2, skip 2 dc, *1 tr in each of next 3 dc, ch 2, skip 2 dc; repeat from * across, ch 3, turn. **Row 3:** 2 dc in center tr of first 3-tr group, ch 1, sc in ch-2 space, ch 1, * 3 dc in center tr of next 3-tr group

A

for shell, ch 1, sc in next ch-2 space, ch 1; repeat from * across, ch 5, turn. **Row 4:** Sc in center dc of first shell, ch 5, * sc in center dc of next shell, ch 5; repeat from * across, ch 5, turn. **Rows 5 through 10:** Sc in ch-5 loop, ch 5, * sc in next loop, ch 5; repeat from * across, ch 5, turn. **Row 11:** 4 dc in first loop, sc in next sc, * 5 dc in next loop, sc in next sc; repeat from * across, fasten off.

JOINING GARMENT SECTIONS

Seams on non-ravel fabrics may be crocheted together rather than stitched, particularly the main seams of a gored skirt or jacket (B). Use knitting worsted, a size G or H crochet hook and a hole puncher. When sections are crocheted together, the fabric edges will not meet. Make a sample first and measure the gap between edges. Cut out sections, omitting seam allowances at edges to be crocheted. Trim away half the gap determined by your sample from each edge to maintain correct fit.

B

Punch holes ¼″ (6 mm) apart, and ⅛″ (3 mm) from edge. Then hold sections with wrong sides together. Working from right to left, insert hook

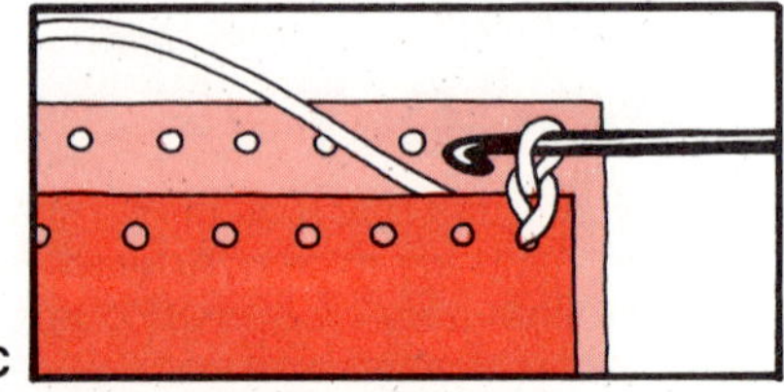
C

D

in first hole of front fabric, from right to wrong side. Draw up a loop of yarn; ch 1 to fasten (C). Insert hook in first hole of back fabric from wrong to right side (D); work 1 hdc. * Insert hook in next hole of front fabric; work 1 hdc. Insert hook in next hole of back fabric; work 1 hdc. Repeat from * to end, fasten yarn and cut (E). Weave ends into wrong side. Press lightly on wrong side with steam iron and press cloth. Apply facings, waistbands, etc. using techniques on pages 33-34.

E

KNITTING

Knitting, another pleasurable and versatile craft, combines very successfully with sewing. If you know the basic knitting stitches, you can substitute knitted sections, like sleeves, yokes, collars or pockets, for fabric ones on sportswear. Or you can add a knitted ruffle to a coverlet or pillow (see ours on page 70). Knitting worsted used with medium-to-heavy fabrics, such as corduroy or tweed, is a good fashion combination.

STITCHES

Stockinette Stitch: (See pocket on the child's sweatshirt shown on page 72). Knit one row, purl one row alternately to create a smooth, untextured area (F).

F

Single Rib: (See lower edge of sleeves on man's jacket, page 71.) On an even number of stitches, knit one, purl one across each row for a narrow, stretchy rib (G). This is used at bottom edge of many sweaters.

G

Double Rib: (See sleeves and pocket of man's jacket, page 71.) On a number of stitches divisible by 4, knit two, purl two across each row, creating a wide rib (A opposite).

A

Quaker Rib: (See the ruffle we added to the round pillow, shown on page 70.) Rows 1, 3, 5, 6, 8, 10: Knit. Rows 2, 4, 7, 9: Purl. Repeat these 10 rows for pattern. This is actually a mock-rib with minimum stretch (B).

B

C

KNITTING A SECTION

For best results, use pattern pieces that are square or rectangular (C), rather than complicated in shape, or knit a straight strip for a ruffle. First, knit a sample swatch to determine your gauge (number of stitches per inch). Next, measure the width of the pattern piece, including seam allowances, or decide on the finished width of the ruffle, adding a seam allowance on one edge. For a pocket that will be applied, omit seam allowances. Then figure the number of stitches that will give the needed width measurement. (Example: If your gauge is 5 stitches per inch and the desired width is 4 inches, 20 stitches will be needed.) If you're going to use Single or Double Rib, allow for the stretchiness of the knit by reducing the finished width by an inch or two (2.5 to 5 cm). Cast on the required stitches and work until the piece measures the same length as the pattern; then bind off. If you are an experienced knitter, shape the piece by increasing or decreasing, but you may have to experiment. Or knit a rectangle, pin pattern piece to it and mark pattern outline with chalk. Staystitch 1/8" (3 mm) inside marked line and trim on marked line.

FINISHING

Press knitted sections lightly on the wrong side with a steam iron and press cloth. To apply a pocket, pin in place and slipstitch it to the garment with matching thread.

To join sleeves to a garment, first machine-stitch the top of the sleeve to the armhole, then sew side and sleeve seams in one step. Pin and baste sections together, stretching the knit and pin-fitting as necessary. Stitch with a slightly loosened tension and a narrow zigzag stitch. Trim the seam allowances to 3/8" (1 cm) and zigzag the edges together. Knitted ruffles may be attached like Edgings, page 63, and seam allowances finished in the same manner as knitted sections.

COLLAGE

Collage is an arrangement of objects attached to a background. Depending on materials, assembly and design, collage can be used as part of a home decorating scheme, like a picture or a pillow, or as a way of adding an unusual touch to a special wardrobe item.

DESIGNS

There are many sources for collage designs—paintings, photographs, greeting cards (D), posters or pieces of needlework. You can reproduce a motif exactly, or you can change and adapt it as desired. For further sources of inspiration, see the array of ideas and photographs in Design Decisions, pages 4 and 5.

MATERIALS

Textiles are a rich source of collage materials. Remnants of fashion and decorator fabrics are excellent starting points. Let your imagination roam freely as you mix colors, prints and textures. Add trims, beads, ribbons, lace or doilies. Use blocks of crochet or knitting, a piece of embroidery, or strands of yarn. Cut up part of an old blanket or quilt. To create dimension and texture, pad, crush or crumple some fabrics, or pull threads to fray the edges. Or use pinking shears to cut out motifs.

D

PREPARATION
Cut the background fabric 2″ (5 cm) larger all around than desired finished size and lightly pencil-mark finished dimensions. For a garment or pillow, do the collage right on the garment or pillow section before seaming. Plan the materials, shapes and placement of your design. As directed on page 7, transfer the design outlines to the background and other fabrics. Then cut out all the shapes.

ASSEMBLY
The way you plan to use the collage will determine how you assemble it. If you're going to frame and hang it, you can use any method—fusing, gluing or stitching. But if you're putting the collage on a garment, you must consider care qualities, what to do with raw edges, and how to attach hard objects like beads or buttons. It's also easier to do collage on one garment section, rather than the assembled garment. Methods for assembling are explained below.

Fusing: You may fuse most fabrics to the background fabric by cutting identical shapes of fusible web and sandwiching them between the motifs and the background fabric. Following the manufacturer's instructions, fuse the motifs in place one layer at a time. Use fusing instead of basting to hold motifs in place for stitching.

Gluing: Fabric glue can be used to attach collage elements, including beads or jewels. For best results, follow manufacturer's instructions.

Stitching: You may stitch collage motifs to the background by hand or machine. First fuse in place; then use hand embroidery or machine stitches to attach motifs, cover raw edges and decorate all at once.

FINISHING
To finish a wall hanging, you can mount the piece on a stretcher or you can frame it. If you've done the collage right on the garment or pillow section, you are now ready to assemble the item in the usual way.

BUTTON ART

As a creative home sewer, you can exploit the decorative, as well as functional, potential of buttons. You probably have lots of buttons on hand, but should you need to buy more, some of the best ones for button decor are small inexpensive "pearl" shirt buttons. Why not arrange buttons decoratively on a vest or skirt (A)? Buttons make excellent collage elements, too. Buttons come in all sizes, shapes and materials, such as mother-of-pearl, plastic, shell, bone, wood and metal. Some antique buttons are even set with semi-precious stones. However, the simplest ones with two or four holes are the best for crafting, since you can use contrasting thread as a creative element in sewing the buttons on. Not all buttons are washable, so keep this in mind when selecting them for a certain garment.

A

B

SEWING BUTTONS
Here are six creative ways to sew on four-hole buttons (B), and you can probably come up with quite a few more. For maximum impact, use contrasting embroidery floss or pearl cotton for sewing. Our button-bedecked vest, page 70, even has a few tassel-tied buttons. The instructions on page 79 tell you how to do them; if you like, a bead can be added before tying the tassel. To save time, you can also sew buttons on with machine zigzag stitching, using contrasting polyester buttonhole twist. Check your machine instruction manual for correct settings, presser foot and procedure to use.

Why not decorate the straps of a handy carryall with a row of buttons? And, add your own button monogram as well (C).

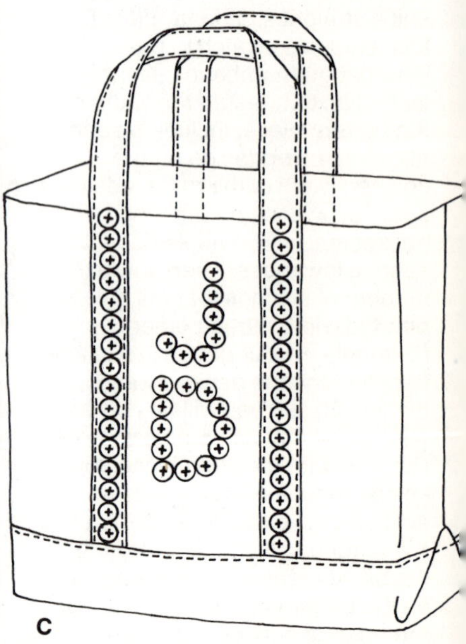
C

PROJECT INSTRUCTIONS

32/PILLOW MAT ♥♥

Shown on page 70
Simplicity 7515, View 3

Materials (for 6 pillows): 8½ yds. (7.80 m) of 45″ (115 cm) canvas, heavy-duty thread, round bolsters.

Directions: 1. Use pattern pieces K and N only. Fold K in half, matching notches. Using small and medium dots on seam line, mark them on fold at same distance from edges; disregard all other small dots. Cut 12 of N and 6 of K; transfer markings to right sides. **2.** Cut 20 strips, each 3 x 12″ (7.6 x 30.5 cm). Turn in long edges and one end ⅝″ (1.5 cm); press; edgestitch. **3.** Attach two ties where marked on 4 pillows only. Assemble pillows, inserting two ties in seams where marked, leaving opening for turning. Turn, stuff, and slipstitch openings.

33/BUTTON-TRIMMED VEST ♥♥♥

Shown on page 70
Simplicity 8013

Materials (for size 10): "Pearl" buttons—**40** ⅝″ (1.5 cm) 4-hole, **59** 7/16″ (1.1 cm) 4-hole and **94** 7/16″ (1.1 cm) 2-hole; 4 colors of embroidery floss; crewel needle.

Directions: (Sew on buttons with 3 strands of floss—2 straight stitches on 2-hole, 2 cross-stitches on 4-hole.)

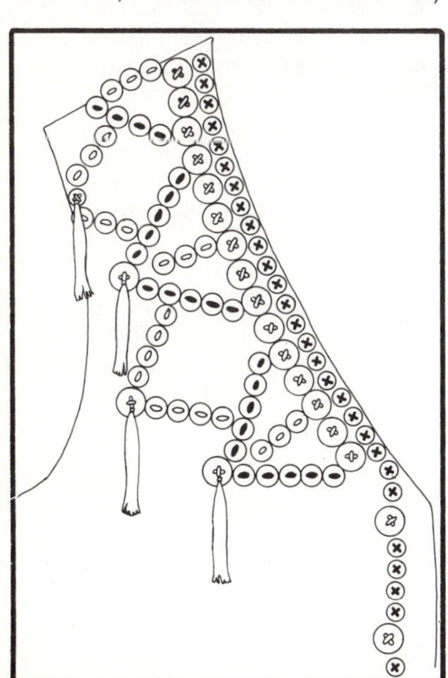

1. Complete vest. **2.** Sew on ⅝″ (1.5 cm) buttons for closure. **3.** From right shoulder seam, sew 4-hole 7/16″ (1.1 cm) buttons along neck edge and down front, with 4 between buttonholes, 2 below last hole. Button vest. **4.** Sew buttons at left neck same way, ending at lap. **5.** Sew ⅝″ (1.5 cm) buttons next to first row at neck, from shoulder seam to above closing. **6.** Sew 2-hole buttons in triangles. At points, sew on 4-hole buttons—7/16″ (1.1 cm) at top point, ⅝″ (1.5 cm) at others—in this way: Cut four 8″ (20.5 cm) lengths of 6-strand floss; with one length, sew in and out of two opposite holes so ends are outside vest; repeat for other two holes; pull threads even and knot; trim ends.

34/EVENING BAG ♥

Shown on page 70
Simplicity 7477

Materials: 5½ yds. (5.05 m) each of three colors of satin cord.

Directions: 1. Cut 26 8″ (20.5 cm) lengths of cord, all colors. Sew bag, enclosing cords in bottom seam (Fringe, page 74). **2.** Knot cords together in two's, close to bag. **3.** For next row, take one cord from first knot and one from 2nd and knot; knot other cord from 2nd with one from 3rd; continue across bag. **4.** For handle, cut two 1¾ yd. (1.60 m) lengths of each color; knot cords together 8″ (20.5 cm) from end. Like colors together, work into flat braid until 8″ (20.5 cm) from end; knot. Tack knot to each side of bag at top, ends hanging free. Trim all ends even.

35/PILLOW WITH KNITTED RUFFLE ♥

Shown on page 70
Simplicity 8138

Materials (for ruffle): 4-oz. skein knitting worsted, size 8 needles.

Directions: Cast on 15 stitches. Work in Quaker Rib (page 77) for 52″ (132 cm); bind off; press. Join ends. Make pillow, inserting ruffle in seam (see Edging, page 63).

36/COLLAGE ♥♥

Shown on pages 70-71

Materials for finished size 30 x 42″ (76 x 107 cm): 1 yd. (0.95 m) of 45″ (115 cm) cotton for backing; cotton solids and prints for shapes; fusible web; white and brown soutache; yarn—yellow, 3 greens, white mohair; thread; canvas stretcher.

Directions: 1. Cut backing 32 x 44″ (81.5 x 112 cm). **2.** Enlarge design and trace. Transfer shapes 1-9 to backing, centering design. Transfer shapes to fabrics; cut out. **3.** Position #'s 1-9 on backing, fuse. Satin-stitch edges. **4.** Place tracing over collage; pin at top. Position #'s 10-24 under tracing; pin. Remove tracing; fuse; satin-stitch edges. **5.** For #24 and #21, place yarn in close rows over shapes; zigzag over yarn (Couching, page 63). For #'s 22, 23 and 11, wind yarn around two fingers; slip off. Place loops to cover shape; stitch through center. **6.** For fence, stitch on white soutache; stitch uprights 1″ (2.5 cm) apart; zigzag ends closely. Stitch on brown soutache to outline silo, barn and X on side. **7.** Tack to stretcher.

Scale: Each square = 3″ (7.6 cm)

37/MAN'S JACKET♥♥

Shown on page 71
Simplicity 7253

Materials: Fabric for jacket without sleeves or pocket (check pattern), four 4-oz. skeins knitting worsted, size 10½ knitting needles.

Directions: (Work with double strand throughout.) **1.** Sleeves (make 2): Cast on 52 stitches; work in Single Rib (page 76) for 3½" (9 cm); continue in Double Rib (page 76) for length of sleeve pattern; bind off. See Knitting a Section, page 77, to cut top of sleeve to shape of pattern.
2. Pockets (make 2): Cast on 24; work in Double Rib for 8" (20.5 cm); bind off. Steam-press; stretch to 6" width. **3.** Sew pockets; leave side edges open 2" (5 cm) above bottoms. Assemble jacket.

38/LADY'S JACKET♥

Shown on page 71
Simplicity 7614

Materials (for 2 closures): Three novelty yarns, about 6 yds. (5.50 m) each; cellophane tape.

Directions: 1. Complete jacket, omitting ties. **2.** Ties (4): For each, cut nine 16" (40.5 cm) strands. Wrap tape around one end; braid. Wrap yarn around braid 2½" (6.3 cm) from other end, knot; trim ends even. Stitch across ends next to tape.
3. Mark fronts 6" (15 cm) and 15" (38 cm) below neck seam, 2½" (6.3 cm) from front edge. **4.** Pin braid ends at mark, taped ends toward edge. Stitch over first stitching; backstitch. Fold braid toward front; slipstitch.

39/SHAGGY RUG♥♥♥

Shown on page 71

Materials: Loosely-woven heavyweight fabric or bedspread, about 50 x 75" (127 x 190.5 cm); eight 4-oz. skeins knitting worsted; latch hook; rug binding.

Directions: 1. Bind fabric edges.
2. Cut yarn into 6" (15 cm) lengths.
3. Using latch hook (page 75), knot clusters of yarn to fabric as desired.

40/MUSHROOM PILLOWS♥♥

Shown on page 72

Materials: Assorted cotton solids and prints, ⅛ to ½ yd. (0.15 to .50 m) each; thread; polyester fiberfill.

Directions: 1. Enlarge and trace each section of pattern. **2.** Cut 2 of each piece, adding ¼" (6 mm) seam allowances. **3.** On inside lines, lap sections and appliqué (see Stitching, page 19). **4.** Right sides together, pin fronts to backs; stitch, leaving opening. **5.** Turn; stuff; slipstitch openings.

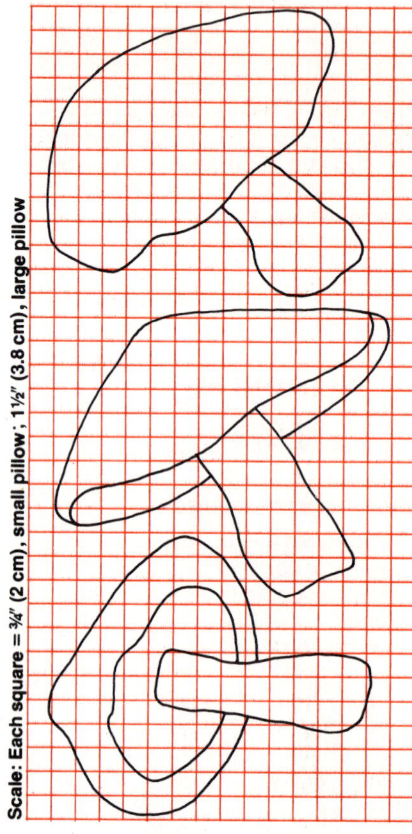

41/CHILD'S SWEATSHIRT♥

Shown on page 72
Simplicity 8121

Materials (pocket): 1 oz. knitting worsted, few yds. yarn in 2 contrasting colors, size 8 knitting needles, tapestry needle, crochet hook.

Directions: 1. Assemble sweatshirt.
2. Pocket: Cast on 40 stitches; work in Stockinette Stitch (page 76) for 6¼" (15.6 cm); bind off; steam press.
3. With first yarn, embroider horse outline (see chart), centered on pocket, in Duplicate Stitch (A).

A

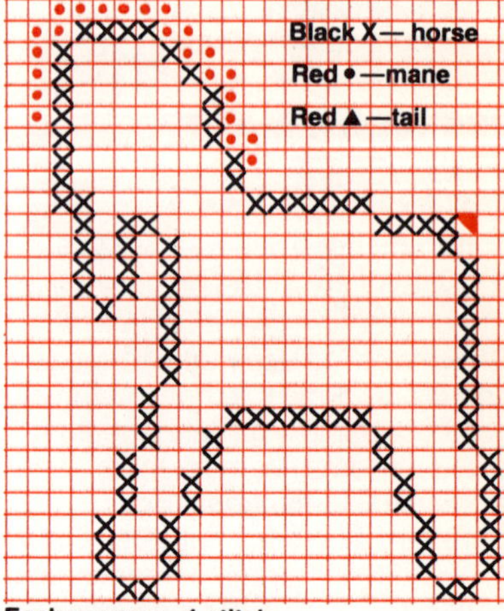

Each square = 1 stitch

4. With 2nd yarn, make a row of Tufting Stitches (page 21) for mane.
5. Tail: cut four 8" (20.5 cm) strands of 2nd yarn; fold in half; insert crochet hook through stitch at tail and pull loop of folded yarn through stitch; draw yarn ends through loop to knot.
6. Sew pocket in place 2½" (6.3 cm) above hem, leaving sides open 1" (2.5 cm) above bottom.

42/CAMISOLE♥♥♥

Shown on page 72
Simplicity 8072

Materials (for ruffle, straps): 2 balls (250 yds. ea.) crochet cotton; no. 7 steel crochet hook, 4½ yds. (4.15 m) ¼" (6 mm) satin ribbon.

Directions: 1. Assemble camisole, omitting straps. Insert 1½ yds. (1.40 m) ribbon through waistline casing.
2. Crochet a 72" (183 cm) ruffle (page 76). Machine-baste along top edge; gather up to fit camisole top, plus 1" (2.5 cm). Cut two 24" (61 cm) lengths of ribbon; pin one to each end of ruffle and weave through holes to center front. **3.** Turn ruffle ends under; stitch to camisole top edge; slipstitch ends. **4.** Straps (make 2): Ch the length of strap pattern.

Row 1: Sc in 2nd ch from hook, ch 1, * 3 dc in next ch, ch 1, sc in next ch, ch 1; repeat from *; fasten thread and cut. **Row 2:** Attach thread to other side of starting ch; work 3 tr in base of first 3-dc group, ch 1, * 3 tr in base of next 3-dc group, ch 1, repeat from *; ch 3, turn. **Row 3:** 2 dc in center tr of first 3-tr group, ch 1, sc in ch-1 space, ch 1, * 3 dc in center tr of next 3-tr group, ch 1, sc in next ch-1 space, ch 1, repeat from *; fasten off. Weave ribbon through holes and secure. Pin to fit; slipstitch.

IDEA FILE

Handcrafted things are fun to do and fun to wear, and the simplest are often the most terrific! Take these, for instance. Each is easy to do, without special equipment, and in minimum time. All can be tackled by a beginner, using techniques from this chapter.

Two simple braids of colorful yarns tie up this trendy head scarf in a stylish manner.♥

Knotted and beaded cord fringe "necklace" is stitched into the yoke seam of jump suit.♥

Play winning tic-tac-toe on a felt game board with boundary lines of bias tape. Stitched-and-stuffed felt playing pieces snap on and off with ease.♥♥

Variation on a theme—braid fabric to create lively home furnishings. Strips of packaged bias tape are braided like a rug and stitched to form decorative placemats.♥♥

Half double crochet gets it all together! Trim seam allowances away, punch holes, crochet together—great for non-ravel fabrics like pseudo-suede.♥♥♥

7511
8059

MIXED MEDIA

CREATE LIVELY LINEUPS

What's the most creative way to sew? By mixing your media, of course! Combine sewing with other artful techniques for fun and great results. Try stenciling, pour-dyeing and painting, along with a dash of appliqué and a smidgen of stitchery, too!

Yummy T-shirt looks good enough to eat. Colorfast felt markers and fake jewels create this delightful treat.♥ **43**

Jumper (or sundress) gets its stripes the easy way—you pour them on right from the bottle, then dye the background.♥♥ **44**

This love-of-a-shawl is a work of art you can wear. Paint the floral spray with colorfast felt markers and add a flip of fringe.♥♥ **45**

His vest of pseudo-suede features stenciled geometric designs both front and back. They're easy and fun to do with colorfast acrylic paint.♥♥ **46**

See how-to's, pages **89-90**

MIXED MEDIA

47 Bold wall hanging combines appliqué, painting and beads.♥♥♥

48 Floral painting on a two-piece dress has the look of water colors.♥♥

49 Painting, embroidery, stitching and stuffing make this lively bull.♥

50 Stenciled motifs are adapted from a Simplicity embroidery design.♥

51 Olé! Paint, stitch and stuff a whole alphabet of pillows.♥♥

Instructions, pages 90-92

8014

MIXED MEDIA

Part of the fun of home sewing is discovering new ways of adding design interest and individuality to the many clothes and home furnishings you sew. One way to do this is to use color in the form of paint or dye and then combine it with other craft techniques, like quilting, fabric mixing or stitch-and-stuff, which we've discussed in previous chapters. By using paints and dyes, you can express any mood—with clear, well-defined stencil shapes, soft, feathery free-hand designs or bold, pour-on stripes. And remember, the more you mix your media, the more fun you'll have and the more creative you'll be!

GENERAL INFORMATION

Painting, stenciling and dyeing don't require a lot of equipment. You can buy paints, brushes and other supplies at any craft shop or art supply store. You'll find dyes at dime stores and supermarkets. Here are some general rules that apply to all techniques for paints and dyes.

- For best results, always read and follow manufacturer's instructions for using a product.

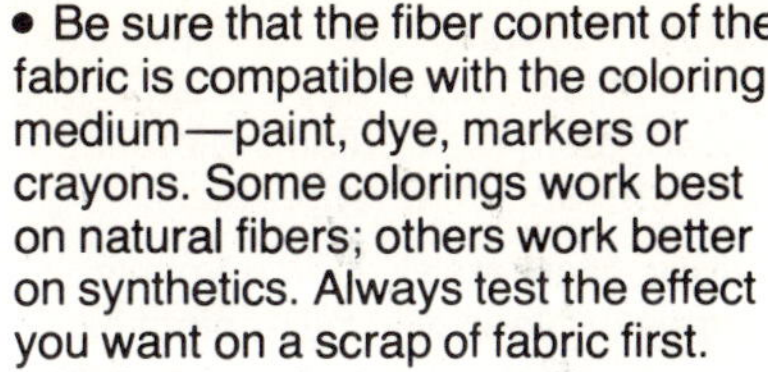

- Be sure that the fiber content of the fabric is compatible with the coloring medium—paint, dye, markers or crayons. Some colorings work best on natural fibers; others work better on synthetics. Always test the effect you want on a scrap of fabric first.
- Make sure that care requirements of fabric and coloring are the same.
- Paint, stencil or dye before you assemble the project.

A

PAINTING

Painting on fabric is a broader term than you might suspect. Ball-point tube painting, crayon transfer, and of course, painting with a brush are all ways to brighten and decorate your sewing projects (A). Just for starters, think about painting your own T-shirt (see ours on page 82). Keep fabric taut as you paint by stretching it over a hoop or canvas stretcher, or by tacking the edges to cardboard.

DESIGNS

Any design meant for appliqué or embroidery may be painted instead. Simplicity has a large selection of transfer designs and fashion patterns that include transfers (A). Or use designs from other sources; Design Decisions, page 5, will tell you where to look. Painting is an ideal way to create striking effects over large areas. For example, you could decorate an entire dress, back of a jacket, or wall hanging with paint. What's more, the fabric painting you do will be completely your own.

MATERIALS

There are many paints and coloring materials on the market. Some of the most popular are described here.

Acrylic Paints: Water-soluble as they come from the tube, all-purpose acrylic paints become permanent when dry and may be washed or dry-cleaned. They come in lots of colors and go on easily with a brush. You'll find they show up best on smooth-surfaced fabrics. The design on the alphabet pillows, page 84, was done with acrylic paints. You can mix acrylic paints on a palette or paper plate for new colors, and you can thin them with water. Paint two thin coats rather than one thick one to cover an area; allow each coat to dry completely before painting over or near it. Some acrylics must be heat-set after painting. Clean up with soap and water.

Fabric Paints: These are similar to the acrylic paints. They usually come packaged in kits containing brushes, a palette and other supplies.

Fabric Markers: Fabric paint also comes in tubes with ball-point tips. With these, you can draw fine lines like the ones on our wall hanging on page 84, do lettering, and make outlines or small details as you would with a pen. And there are felt-tip markers made for use on fabrics. The delicate floral design on the shawl, pages 82-83, was done with this type of marker. The colors can be washed or dry-cleaned.

Crayon Transfer: Use wax crayons made for fabrics to draw your design in reverse on paper; then place the crayoned side face down and iron the design onto fabric. This method works best on synthetic fibers. Or, try non-waxy pastel crayons which may be used to draw a design directly on the fabric. To make the color permanent, simply press the design with a hot iron.

Sparkle Color: Draw a design with clear glue and sprinkle with glitter, or buy glue ready-mixed with glitter for sparkling designs in one easy step.

CREATIVE IDEAS

- "Put your name in lights" on a belt or make a glittering design on an evening dress by combining sparkle color and ball-point tube paints.
- Paint a pots-and-pans or wooden-utensils motif on a tablecloth or kitchen curtains.
- Make games and sports the theme on painted throw pillows, curtains or fabric murals for a young boy's room.

STENCILING

Stenciling is one more example of an ancient art that fits in so well with our contemporary life-style. Just cut out a design motif from heavy paper, place it over fabric and apply paint over the cut-out. Remove the paper and voilà! There's your design. Make a single bold motif, or for a band or border, repeat the motif. You can stencil fashions, accessories or home furnishings, like our placemats inspired by a folkloric theme, page 84. Do a border around the hem of a skirt or tablecloth. Stencil closet accessories with names of stored items. Create fake pockets on a teenager's T-shirt.

DESIGNS

Any uncomplicated motif can be used for stenciling. Even elaborate shapes can be modified or broken down into simpler components for easy stenciling. For example, you could trace a drawing of a flower and then separate the petals, leaves and stems with a bit of space (A).

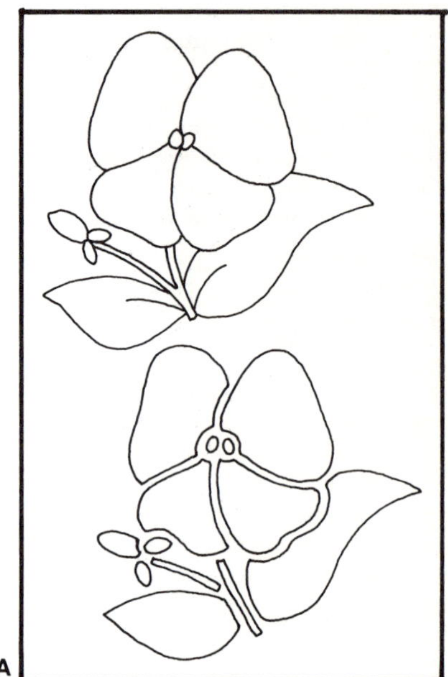

A

You can also purchase a variety of ready-to-use stencils. Among these are alphabets in many styles and sizes, as well as florals and other designs from nature. Ready-to-use stencils are usually made of heavy paper or clear acetate. The latter is washable, so you can clean it off periodically and re-use it.

EQUIPMENT

If you're making your own stencils, you'll need pencils and a marking pen, tracing paper, carbon paper, illustration board (a lightweight, smooth-surfaced cardboard), stencil paper (a semi-transparent, heavy waxed paper), tape, metal-edged ruler and a craft knife.

Acrylic paints, described on page 85, are ideal for stenciling. Stencil brushes have blunt, fairly stiff bristles and are available in several sizes. Clean them with soap and water and allow them to dry with the bristles facing down. It's a good idea to keep a supply of newspapers on hand to protect work surfaces; paper plates are great for mixing paints and easy clean-up.

MAKING THE STENCIL

Once you've chosen your design and separated it as described, you can prepare your stencil. Using carbon paper and a pencil as directed in Design Decisions, page 7, transfer your design to a sheet of illustration board. Then trace over the transferred design with a black marking pen to make it highly visible (B). Now tape a sheet of stencil paper over the traced design and cut it out with a craft knife. Hold the knife vertically and be sure it has a fresh, sharp blade. Cut each line with one clean stroke, just cutting through the stencil paper (C). Use a ruler to guide the knife for making straight cuts. When cutting curves or circles, hold the knife in one hand and turn the illustration board with your other hand as you cut. Cut out smaller shapes first, then proceed to the larger ones. To cut two identical stencils at the same time, you can tape two layers of stencil paper over the design. Then cut through both layers, using slightly heavier pressure.

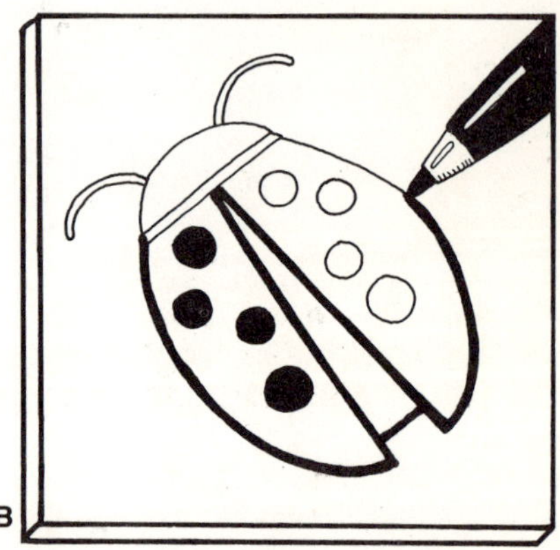

B

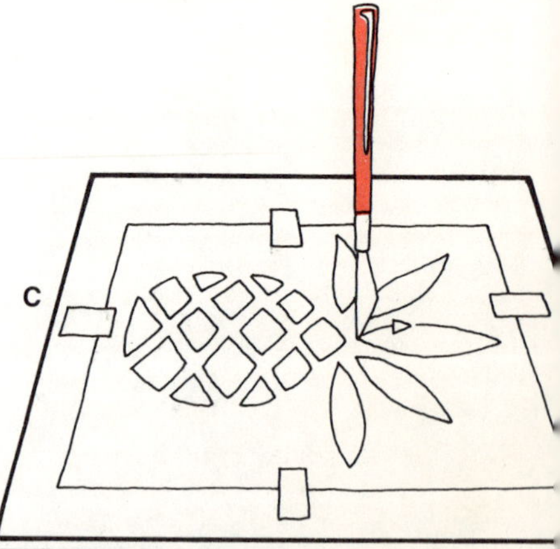

C

STENCILING METHODS

Spread the fabric to be stenciled on a flat surface. Tack or tape the edges down to keep the fabric smooth. Place the stencil over the fabric and tape the corners. Squeeze a dab of paint onto a paper plate and dip the tip of the brush into

A

it; do not load the brush with too much paint. Remove any excess paint from the brush on newspaper before you begin. Then, holding the brush vertically, apply the paint with an up-and-down motion; do not stroke, dab. To hold the edges of the stencil down on the fabric, use the point of a pencil held in your free hand (A). If it is necessary to apply a second coat of paint to cover an area completely, keep the stencil taped in position while drying. Be sure to let the first coat dry completely before starting the second. When you have finished applying the paint, remove the tape and lift the stencil carefully to prevent the paint from smudging.

Separate Stencils: Some designs consist of various shapes done in several different colors. With such a design, it's easier to cut a separate stencil for all the shapes to be done with each color (B, C). Our placemat and napkin on page 84 were painted with separate stencils.

First trace your design as usual onto illustration board. Then draw two small shapes (triangles, for example) on opposite sides of the board 1 to 2″ (2.5 to 5 cm) away from the design (B, C). These shapes are called registration marks; they will help you line up the design on each of the separate stencils.

Now cut a separate stencil for each color, cutting out the registration marks, too. When you tape the first stencil to the fabric, do not paint through the registration marks; instead, fill them in with tailor's chalk. Then, when you use succeeding stencils, you can line up the

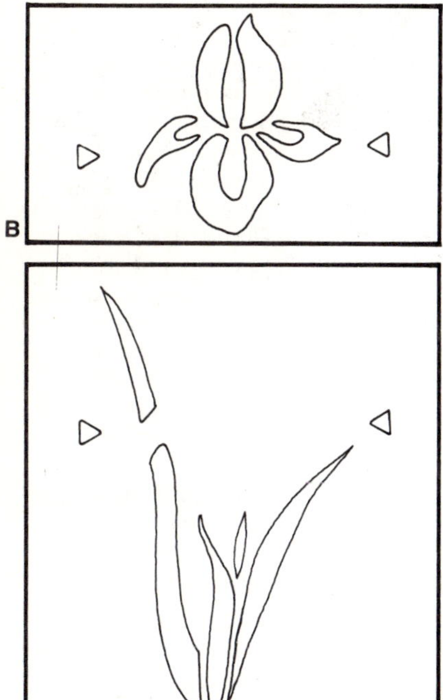
B

C

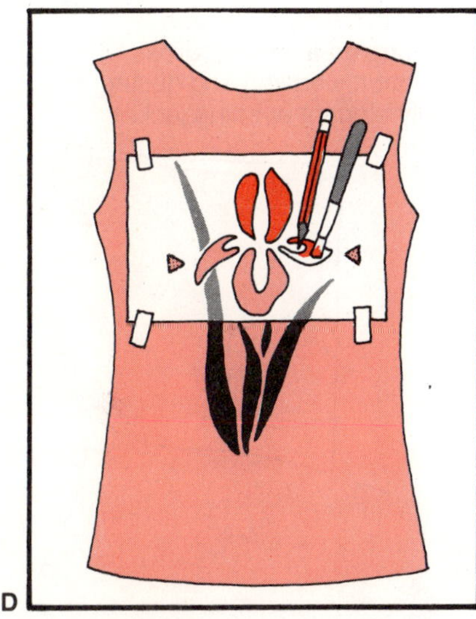
D

registration marks with the chalk marks to insure that your design is properly aligned (D). Let each color dry before going on to the next one.

POUR-ON DYEING

Pour-on dyeing is an interesting variation of tie-dyeing. With this method, you pour stripes of liquid dye right onto your fabric. You then tie off the stripes before immersing the fabric in a dye bath. When you remove the ties, the tied-off areas, which resist the background dye, form their own contrasting design. On page 82, you'll find our colorful jumper-sundress featuring chevroned pour-dyed stripes.

EQUIPMENT

You'll need both liquid and powdered dyes; plastic squeeze bottles for applying the liquid dye (the bottles used for hair coloring are best); string or rubber bands for tying; two large pots; long-handled tongs; and a large spoon for stirring. You should also have some plastic sheeting to protect your work surface, and a damp sponge to wipe up spatters and spills.

FABRICS

Fabrics for pour-on dyeing **must** be washable. Since natural fibers are more receptive to dye than some synthetics, choose a fabric that contains at least 50% natural fiber. Make a test swatch first to determine how well the color will be absorbed. Lightweight fabrics are more satisfactory than heavy or densely-woven ones. A thin, soft 100% cotton fabric is ideal for pour-on dyeing. Always wash items made from home-dyed fabric separately in cool to lukewarm water and mild soap or detergent. Never use bleach. Be sure to dry them away from direct sunlight.

PROCEDURE

Before you start the actual pour-dyeing, you should think about colors and how you can use them most effectively in your project.

Color Schemes: Generally, pour-on dyeing is done with two or three contrasting colors—one or two dark colors for stripes and a lighter color for the background, or vice versa. For example, you might choose complementary colors—orange stripes with a dark blue background, or yellow stripes with a deep violet background for pour-dyeing.

How to Dye: If the fabric is new or soiled, wash it. Otherwise, wet it thoroughly and wring out. Transfer the liquid dye to squeeze bottles. Spread the wet fabric on a protected surface. Now squeeze lines of liquid dye over the fabric, making sure the dye penetrates fabric completely (A). The dye will spread on the fabric. Lines may run in any direction as long as they are roughly parallel; they may be wide or narrow. Now gather up fabric along dye lines (B) and tie off each colored area tightly with rubber bands or string (C).

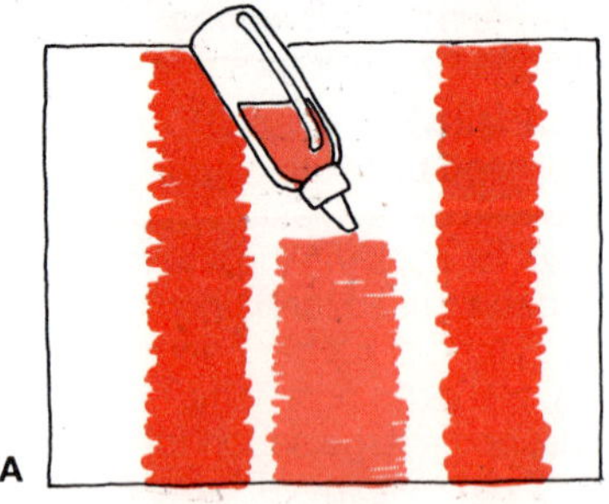

A

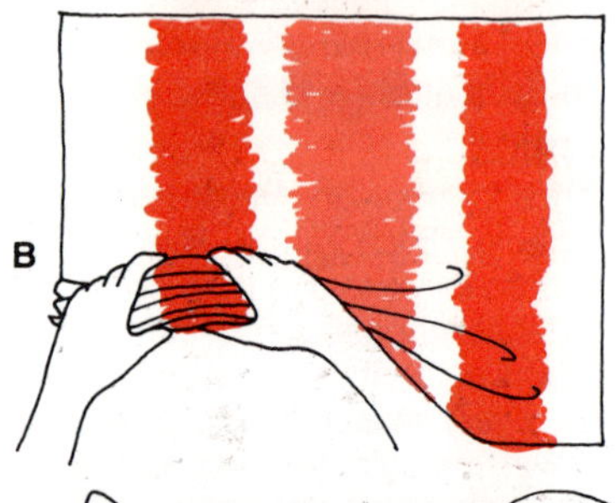

B

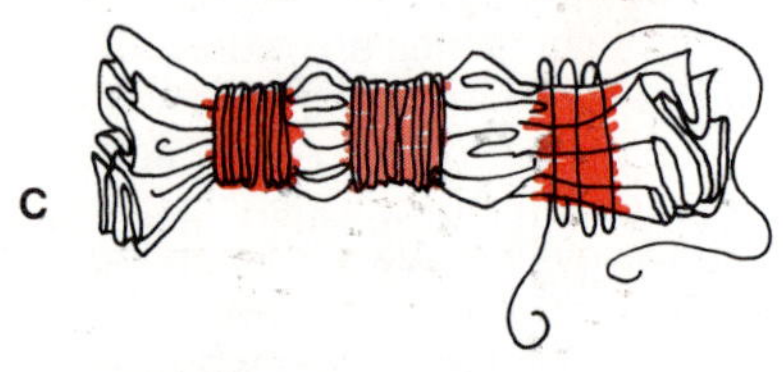

C

Following the manufacturer's instructions, mix powdered dye with water in a large pot. Fill another pot with clear water for rinsing. Place fabric in dye pot and simmer slowly over low heat for 20 minutes, turning occasionally with large spoon. With tongs, remove fabric from dye, transfer to clear water and simmer for another 20 minutes. If necessary, change rinse water and continue to simmer until water is fairly clear. Rinse fabric in cold water. Remove ties, rinse again and allow fabric to drip-dry away from direct sunlight.

CREATIVE IDEAS

Use tie-dyed fabric to make casual clothes—shirts, pants, long skirts and scarves (D). Make a throw pillow with a chevron design. Pour dye on in a V, then fold fabric in half at points of V's and gather up along each stripe (E). Tie off, then dye background and complete pillow.

MORE MIXED MEDIA

Put on your creative thinking cap! You're sure to come up with lots of ideas of your own for combining some of the many techniques we've talked about. Remember, design and care compatibility are very important. To make an elegant impression, choose luxurious fabrics and stylish techniques. Our satin jacket, page 95, with trapunto and hand embroidery, is a perfect illustration of this principle. Or if you're in the mood for fun, mix some light-hearted techniques, as in our bull pillow, page 84. He combines stitch-and-stuff, painting, hand embroidery, and knotting.

Here are some more combinations:

- Fabric mixing, patchwork and trims on a tablecloth, or fashion item.
- Stenciling and braiding on a carryall or tote bag.
- Pour-dyeing, trims and knotting on a tunic or dress.
- Ribbon weaving and quilting for a really elegant evening jacket.

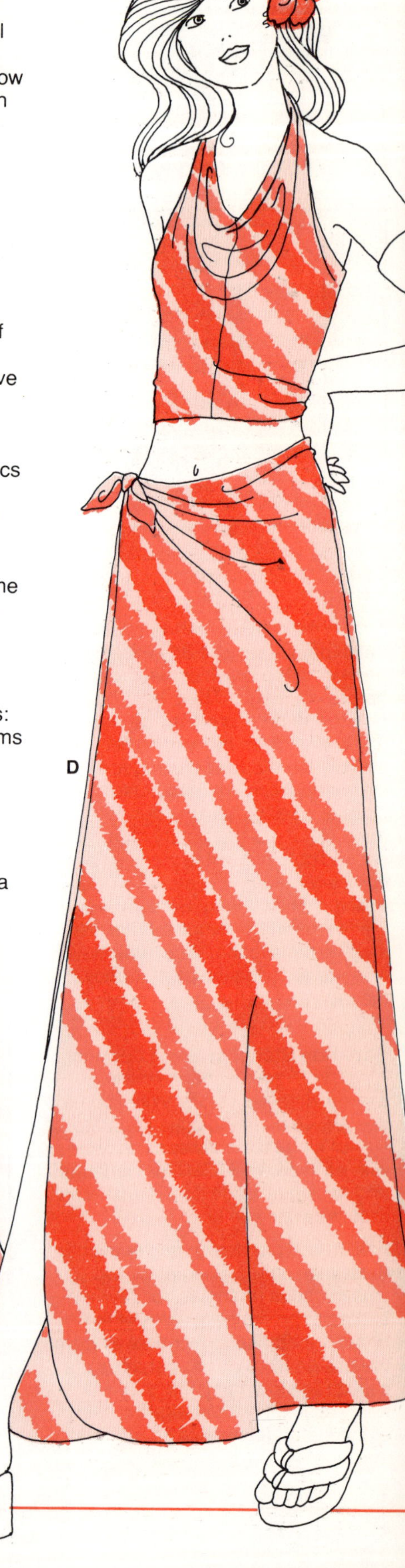

D

E

PROJECT INSTRUCTIONS

43/CHILD'S T-SHIRT♥

Shown on page 82
Simplicity 7511

Materials: Light blue, lime, pink and black colorfast felt-tip markers; assorted multi-colored glue-on "jewels"; fabric glue.

Directions: 1. Cut out T-shirt. **2.** Enlarge ice cream cone design. Transfer to front, placing top edge of ice cream 1½″ (3.8 cm) below neck edge. **3.** Place brown paper under T-shirt. Fill in the scoops of ice cream first—lime on top, pink in the middle and blue on the bottom. With black, draw scoop and cone outlines and crisscross lines. **4.** Glue "jewels" to ice cream as desired; using red "jewels," put a cherry on top. **5.** Assemble T-shirt.

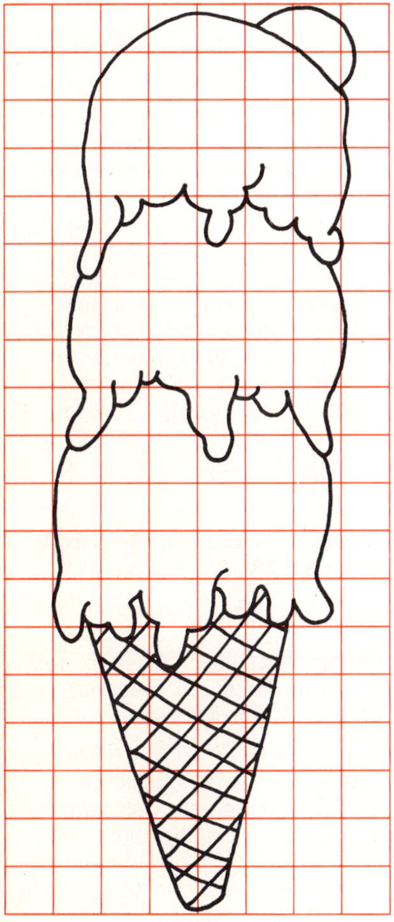

Scale: Each square = ⅝″ (1.5 cm)

44/POUR-DYED DRESS♥♥

Shown on page 82
Simplicity 8059

Materials: Lightweight unbleached muslin for dress; 1 box of coral powdered fabric dye; 1 bottle each of kelly green and navy blue liquid fabric dye; see equipment, page 87.

Directions: 1. Prepare fabric as directed on pages 87-88. Cut out dress. Line up side edges of dress sections, right front to right back and left front to left back. Mark each piece at side edge 2″ (5 cm) and 6″ (15 cm) above hemline.
2. Transfer liquid dye to squeeze bottles. Rinse all dress sections in water and wring out. On work space, place both dress front sections together with front edges matching. Use yard stick to guide your hand as you pour, placing it about ½″ (1.3 cm) from desired line. Starting at center front 1″ (2.5 cm) below top edge, pour a line of green dye diagonally across one front section to 6″ (15 cm) mark at lower side edge. Beginning 5″ (12.5 cm) from top, pour a parallel line of blue dye, ending at side edge mark 2″ (5 cm) above hemline. Repeat for other front section. Clean off work surface and carefully turn both sections over. Redraw the dye lines on the reversed side, following the first set of lines. Gather the fabric along the dye lines and tie off each color and area between lines with rubber bands. **3.** Draw dye lines on back sections as for front, and tie off. **4.** Pour a line of green dye lengthwise down center of all strap sections; turn over and repeat. Gather along dye lines and tie. **5.** Following instructions on page 88, dye all dress sections coral. When dyeing is complete, let dry; then assemble and finish dress.

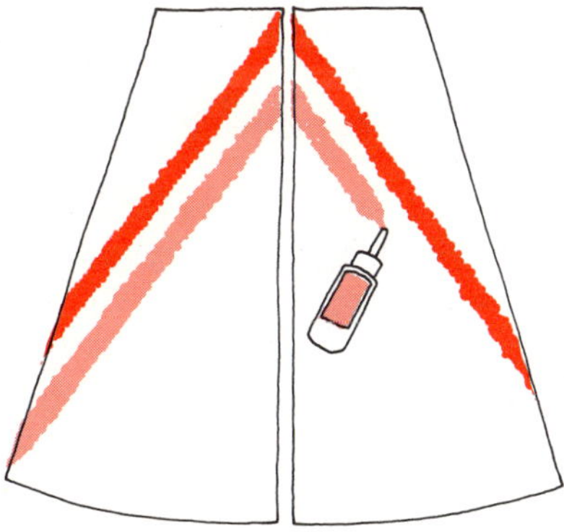

45/PAINTED SHAWL♥♥

Shown on pages 82-83
Simplicity 7332

Materials: Lightweight fabric for shawl and self-lining; 2¾ yards (2.55 m) rayon fringe; red, orange, blue and green colorfast felt-tip markers.

Directions: 1. Cut out shawl and lining. Enlarge and transfer design to right side of shawl (reverse to make second half), or paint design freehand. **2.** With red, paint bow, starting with darkest areas and working toward lighter areas. Leave some areas uncolored to suggest highlights. **3.** With orange, paint flowers and buds, working from outside of petals toward center. Make blue dots at centers by dabbing lightly with a corner of the marker tip. **4.** With green, paint stems, using light, quick strokes to produce thin lines. Do not paint over knot of bow, but continue green stems below knot. **5.** Paint leaves, working from stem end to tips. **6.** Pin shawl and lining right sides together, enclosing fringe in seam (as for Edging Inserted in Seam on page 63). Stitch a ⅝″ (1.5 cm) seam all around, leaving an opening for turning. Turn right side out, slipstitch opening and press edges.

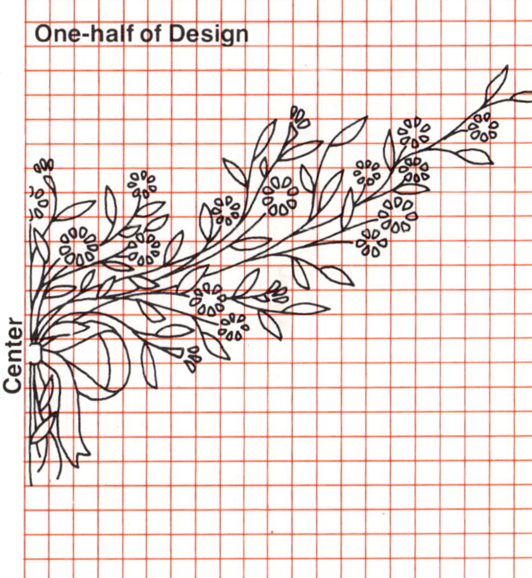

Scale: Each square = 1¼″ (3.2 cm)

46/STENCILED VEST♥♥

Shown on page 83

Simplicity 7701

Materials: Dark and light blue acrylic paint; supplies for stencil making (see page 86); small paintbrush.

Directions: 1. Complete vest. **2.** Enlarge designs and trace each onto stencil paper four times, reversing design to make two complete stencils; cut out as directed on page 86. **3.** Tape dark blue stencil to right front of vest, following vest edge markings; paint with dark blue. Do not paint large triangle. Repeat for left front of vest. **4.** Tape light blue stencil to right front of vest, matching registration marks; paint with light blue. Do not paint large triangle. Paint left front the same way. **5.** Use paintbrush to paint in light and dark blue triangle and stripes by hand; use stencil edge as guide and see photo, page 83, for design guide. **6.** If desired, stencil the area of design with squares in light and dark blue near bottom of V-neckline.

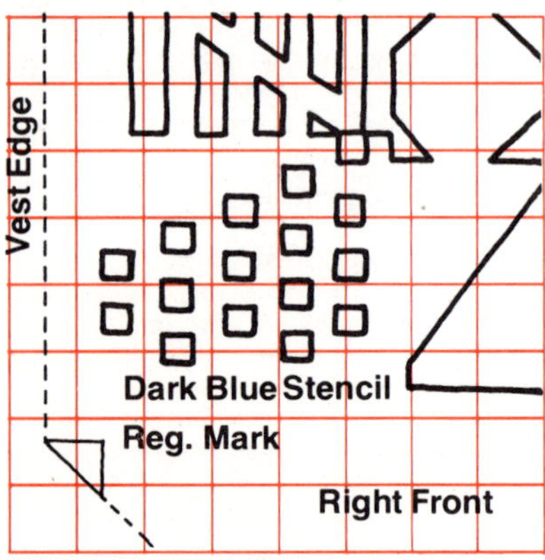

One Quarter of Design

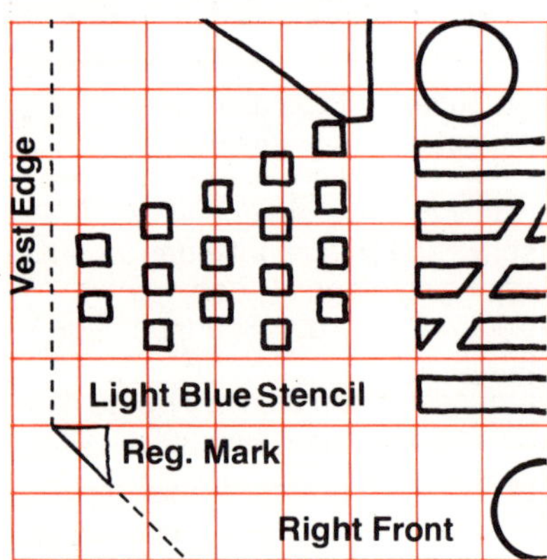

One Quarter of Design

Scale: Each square = ½″ (1.3 cm)

Scale: Each square = 1¾″ (4.5 cm)

47/WALL HANGING♥♥♥

Shown on page 84

Materials: Medium-weight cotton fabric 45″ (115 cm) wide—⅞ yard (.80 m) shocking pink, ⅓ yard (30.5 cm) red and bright blue, ¾ yard (.70 m) green, ½ yard (.50 m) white, ¼ yard (.25 m) yellow; 12 black ⅜″ (1 cm) buttons; fusible web; matching thread; black fine-point marking pen; polyester fiberfill stuffing; ¼″ (6 mm) foamboard, 26 x 30″ (66 x 76 cm).

Directions: 1. Enlarge design. Trace design twice. On one tracing, cut out each piece. **2.** For #1, cut pink fabric in rectangle 26½ x 30½″ (67.3 x 77.3 cm). Cut other pieces using tracing as follows: #2, red; #7, blue; #'s 5, 8, 11, 12, 13, 14, 15 and 16, green; #'s 9 and 10, yellow; and #'s 3, 4, 6, and 17, white. Cut fusible web for each piece, except #17. **3.** Place the uncut tracing over #1, centering design; pin along three sides. Slip #'s 2-6 under tracing and pin in place. Remove tracing and fuse pieces. Satin-stitch around each piece with matching thread. After each set of pieces is fused and stitched, replace tracing. Draw design on #7 with marking pen, following diagram. Position #'s 7-11, overlapping them slightly on preceding pieces; fuse and satin-stitch. Repeat for #'s 12-16. Pin #17 in place (do not fuse); satin-stitch. Slash the back an inch under the flower and push in stuffing with a pencil until flower is very puffy. Slipstitch opening. **4.** Sew on buttons, following photo, page 84, for placement. **5.** Turn under ¼″ (6 mm) on rectangle sides and press. Stretch over foamboard edges; insert pins ½″ (1.3 cm) apart, straight down into edges.

48/PAINTED TWO-PIECE DRESS♥♥

Shown on page 84

Simplicity 8014

Materials: Lightweight silk or cotton for dress; white, red, magenta, green and yellow acrylic fabric paint; fine and wide sable brushes.

Directions: 1. Cut out skirt front section and mark tuck placement. Enlarge design and position under front with design close to right side seam, and lowest part slightly above highest tuck; pin.
2. Work on a protected surface. Use white, green and red paints from

Scale: Each square = 2″ (5 cm)

jars. Mix others as follows: for pink and deep pink—white with magenta; pale green—yellow with green; orange—yellow with red. **3.** Paint colors, following design under fabric and using photo on page 84 as color guide. Complete dress.

49/BULL PILLOW♥

Shown on page 84
Simplicity 8138

Materials: Turquoise fabric for pillow, plus 1/4 yard (0.25 m) for legs and head; 1/8 yard (0.15 m) each yellow, green and red fabric; matching thread; lavender and orange felt; black six-strand embroidery floss; orange crewel yarn; bright orange rug yarn; white and rust acrylic paint; fabric glue; stuffing for pillow and head.

Directions: 1. Body: Cut out pillow front and back. Cut 3 yellow and 2 green strips 14½ x 3″ (36.8 x 7.6 cm); turn under ½″ (1.3 cm) on long edges; press. Pin strips to front in alternating colors, 1¼″ (3.2 cm) apart; edgestitch. **2.** Legs: Cut four 4 x 6″ (10 x 15 cm) turquoise strips. Fold in half lengthwise, right sides together; stitch ¼″ (6 mm) from side and bottom edges, leaving top open. Turn and stuff. Stitch across opening ¼″ (6 mm) from edge. Paint rust hooves on legs 1″ (2.5 cm) high. Pin legs to right side of front with top of leg on pillow seam allowance, two at head end, 1″ (2.5 cm) apart, and two at tail end, 1″ (2.5 cm) apart; machine-baste along pillow seam line. Stitch front to back, leaving an opening for turning. Turn and stuff; slipstitch opening. **3.** Head: Enlarge and trace head; add ¼″ (6 mm) seam allowance. Cut 2 from turquoise. Trace (add seams) and cut 2 red horn sections. Stitch bottom of horns to head front and back. Stitch front and back of head together, leaving opening. Turn, stuff and slipstitch opening. Paint white eyes and nose. With 6 strands of floss, embroider centers of eyes with overcast stitch, outline eyes with chain and straight stitch, and mouth and line between horns with stem stitch (see pages 46-47). Cut two lavender triangles and two orange circles and glue to head as shown. Slipstitch head to pillow body. **4.** Beard: Thread 10″ (25.5 cm) strand of crewel yarn through needle, take a stitch through chin; remove needle. With ends even, tie knot under chin. Repeat with 2 more strands. **5.** Tail: Hold five 20″ (51 cm) strands of rug yarn together, fold in half and tie knot near fold. Sew to corner of pillow.

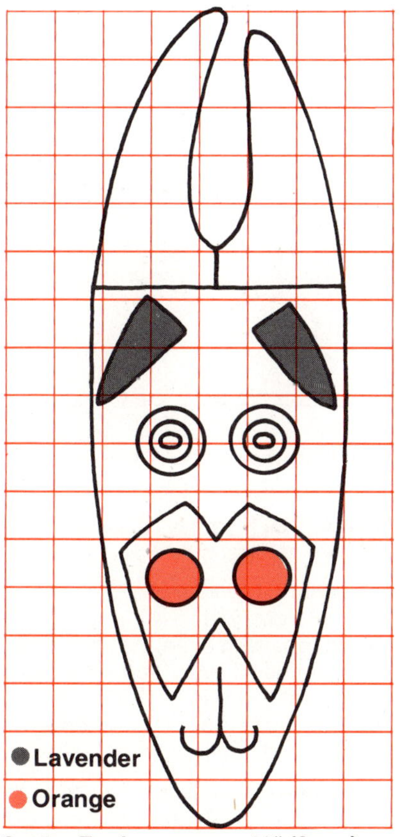

Scale: Each square = ¾″ (2 cm)

50/STENCILED PLACEMAT AND NAPKIN♥

Shown on page 84
Simplicity 6439

Materials: 13½ x 17½″ (34.3 x 44.3 cm) placemats; 16″ square (40.5 cm) napkins; red, orange, yellow, green, turquoise acrylic paints; supplies for stencil making (see page 86).

Directions: 1. Separating and simplifying the sections of the design, trace and cut a separate stencil for each color as described on pages 86 and 87, using photo on page 84 as color guide. **2.** Place stencils 1½″ (3.8 cm) from one corner of placemat and 1″ (2.5 cm) from one corner of napkin. Paint each color section, following instructions on page 87; allow paint color to dry before starting to apply a new one.

51/PAINTED ALPHABET PILLOWS♥♥

Shown on page 84
Simplicity 8139

Materials: Yellow fabric for pillows; white, blue, green, red and violet acrylic paints; small paintbrush.

Directions: 1. Cut out pillows. Enlarge designs (below and next page); transfer to pillow fronts, extending and repeating motifs to fill entire area. **2.** Paint designs, using photo on page 84 as color guide; let yellow fabric show through as part of design. Apply two coats and allow each color to dry before starting next color. **3.** When dry, finish pillows.

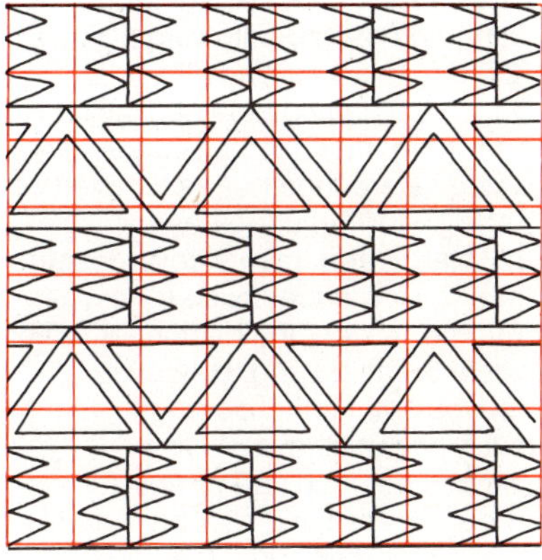

Scale: Each square = 1″ (2.5 cm)

Scale: Each square = 1″ (2.5 cm)

52/TRAPUNTO JACKET♥♥♥

Shown on page 95
Simplicity 7956

Materials (for size 10-12) Jacket fabric plus ½ yard (0.50 m) extra, lining fabric (same yardage as for jacket), polyester batting and fiberfill, 2 yards (1.85 m) ⅛″ (3 mm) cording, 1 ounce (28 g) 4-ply yarn, 1 skein six-strand embroidery floss, plastic yarn needle, large darning needle, tracing paper.

Directions: 1. Cut jacket fabric, lining and batting, allowing 1″ (2.5 cm) extra around all edges. Sandwich batting between jacket and lining, matching all edges; pin. Baste layers together as directed on page 20 for Securing Layers.
2. Enlarge and trace sleeve design onto tracing paper twice (one in reverse), extending design for larger sizes. **3.** Pin tracing to sleeves (leaves point to right on right sleeve, to left on left sleeve). Using 8 stitches per inch (2.5 cm), stitch through paper and all fabric layers over all marked lines; tear away tracings. **4.** Stuff bottom half of each leaf as directed in Free-Form Trapunto, page 45. **5.** Using double strand of yarn in darning needle, stuff stems as described in Channel Trapunto, page 45. **6.** Using cording in plastic needle, stuff the channels at top of design. **7.** Enlarge and trace designs for jacket (one in reverse); pin to jacket fronts and stitch over designs as for sleeves. **8.** Stuff one half of each leaf, petals and centers of each flower, and stems as for sleeves. **9.** With 2 strands of floss in needle, fill in centers of flowers with rows of chain stitch (page 46).
10. Assemble jacket, substituting self-fabric bias strips for foldover braid and ties. Cut, join and apply bias strips as described on page 35.

Sleeve Design

Scale: Each square = 1½″ (3.8 cm)

Jacket Right Front

Each square = 1¼″ (3.2 cm)

53/QUILT♥♥♥

Shown on pages 94-95

Materials: Medium-weight cotton 45″ (115 cm) wide—4 yds. (3.70 m) white (or a twin sheet), 2 yds. (1.85 m) lavender, ⅞ yd. (0.80 m) green, ⅓ yd. (30.5 cm) blue; polyester batting; white, lavender, green and blue thread, tracing paper.

Directions for finished coverlet 70″ L x 41½″ W (178 x 105.3 cm): **1.** Cut white rectangle 71½ x 43″ (181.8 x 109 cm). **2.** Enlarge diagram for appliqué design and trace. Transfer design to fabric and cut border and petal centers of lavender, iris flowers of blue, and stems and leaves of green. **3.** Place tracing over rectangle, centering it. Pin border, stems and leaves under tracing. Satin-stitch around edges with matching thread. After groups of pieces are pinned in place, remove tracing; after stitching, replace tracing. Pin flowers; satin-stitch. Pin all of petal centers in place; satin-stitch. **4.** Cut backing from white fabric 72 x 44″ (183 x 112 cm). Center top and batting over backing. Baste as directed on page 20. Quilt through all three layers, just outside of satin-stitching, using straight stitch and matching color thread. Bind top with backing as for Quilts on page 21.

Scale: Each square = 4″ (10 cm)

IDEA FILE

If one is good, more are better . . . definitely applies to our special Mixed Media techniques. Here, we present a few more possibilities for ingeniously combining the needle arts with the visual arts—painting, dyeing, stenciling, buttons. Try them for creative pleasure and fashion excitement!

Stencil a fabric window shade with a cheerful design adapted from the view outside your window on a sunny day. ♥

Transform a Jiffy® skirt—paint a colorful rainbow on unbleached muslin. Use fabric paint to create this lovely illusion. ♥

A Jiffy® top makes a perfect palette for the pour-on method of tie-dyeing. First create the design, then dye the background. ♥♥♥

8017

8158

7698
7116

Decorate a denim jacket with a proud eagle. He's done in true Mixed Media style—machine-appliqué, buttons and a dab of paint. ♥♥

The duffle bag—spell it out for all the world to see with fabric paint and stencil letters. ♥

7867

GRAND FINALE

We've saved the best for last! Now that you've seen all the great projects in this book, you'll be dazzled by these two gems. Both are glorious ways to Sew Something Special!

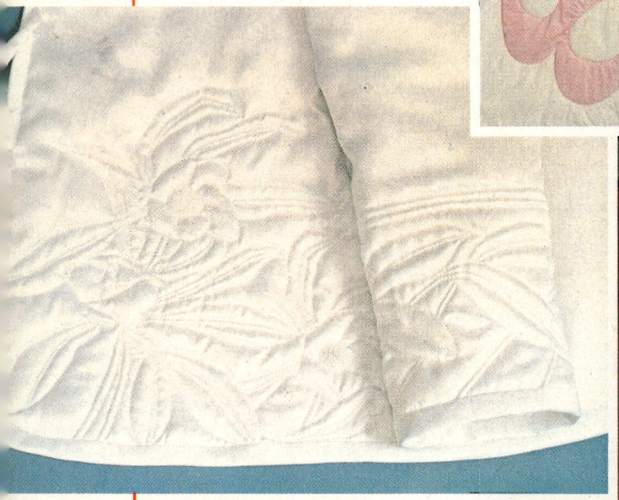

52 Luxury reaches new heights in this stunning

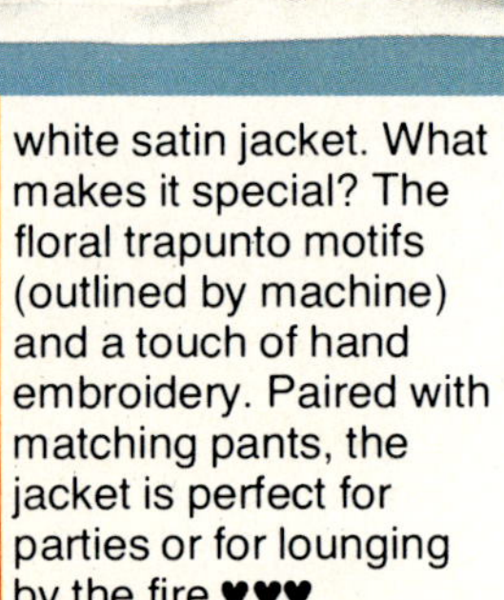

white satin jacket. What makes it special? The floral trapunto motifs (outlined by machine) and a touch of hand embroidery. Paired with matching pants, the jacket is perfect for parties or for lounging by the fire.♥♥♥

53 Spring flowers bloom forever on this nostalgic coverlet. The curvy *art-nouveau* design recalls an earlier, elegant era. But the method is strictly up-to-date—the appliqués and the outline quilting are all done by machine.♥♥♥

Instructions, page 92

7956
7959

INDEX:

Bold numbers indicate color photos.